THE GLOBAL GRILL

KATHLEEN SLOAN

Robert
ROSE

The Global Grill

For complete cataloguing information, see page 6.

DESIGN, EDITORIAL AND PRODUCTION:	MATTHEWS COMMUNICATIONS DESIGN INC.
PHOTOGRAPHY:	MARK T. SHAPIRO
ART DIRECTION/FOOD PHOTOGRAPHY:	SHARON MATTHEWS
FOOD STYLIST:	KATE BUSH
PROP STYLIST:	CHARLENE ERRICSON
RECIPE EDITORS/TEST KITCHEN:	JAN MAIN/RIKI DIXON/LESLEIGH LANDRY
MANAGING EDITOR:	PETER MATTHEWS
INDEXER:	BARBARA SCHON
COLOR SCANS & FILM:	POINTONE GRAPHICS

We acknowledge the financial support of the Government of Canada through the Book Publishing Industry Development Program (BPIDP) for our publishing activities.

Canadä

Published by: Robert Rose Inc. • 156 Duncan Mill Road, Suite 12
Toronto, Ontario, Canada M3B 2N2 Tel: (416) 449-3535

Printed in Canada

1234567 BP 02 01 00 99

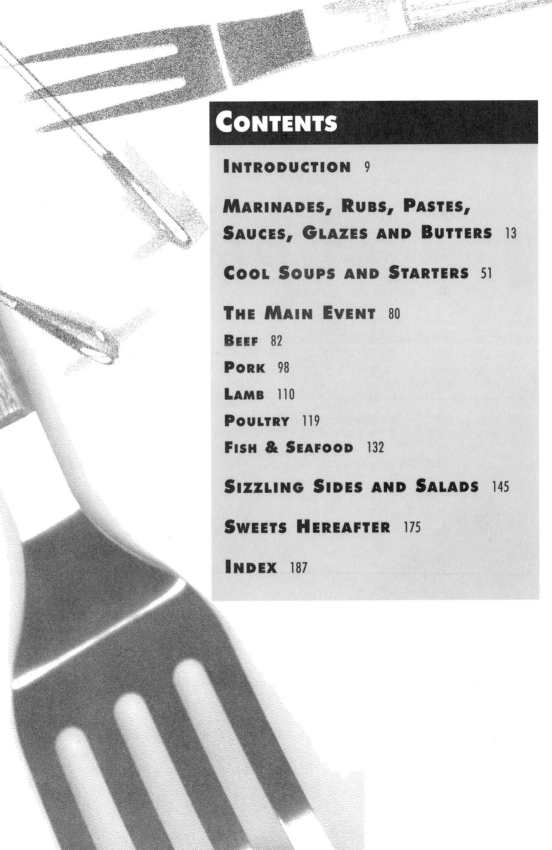

CONTENTS

INTRODUCTION 9

MARINADES, RUBS, PASTES, SAUCES, GLAZES AND BUTTERS 13

COOL SOUPS AND STARTERS 51

THE MAIN EVENT 80
BEEF 82
PORK 98
LAMB 110
POULTRY 119
FISH & SEAFOOD 132

SIZZLING SIDES AND SALADS 145

SWEETS HEREAFTER 175

INDEX 187

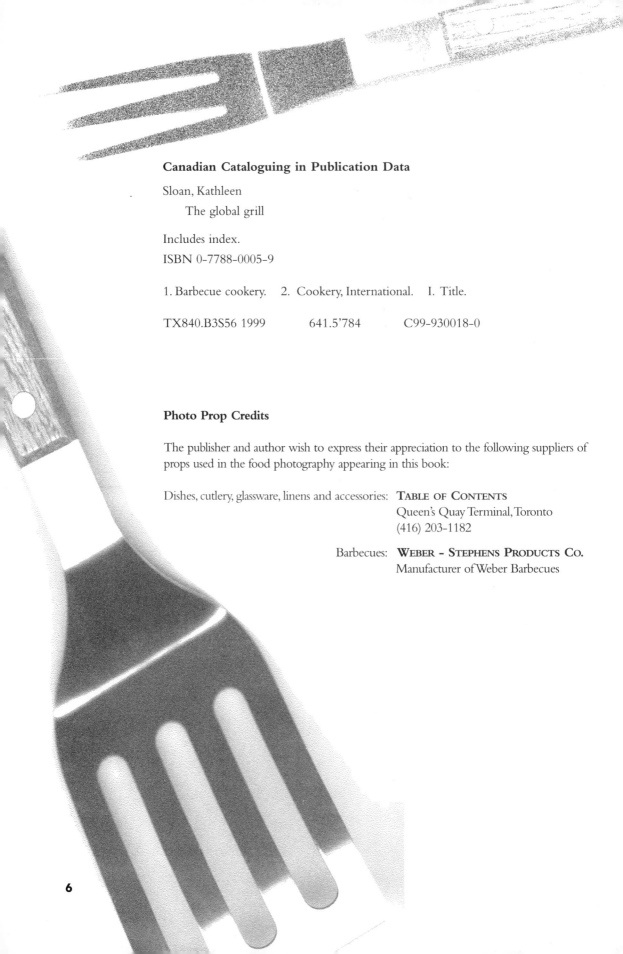

Canadian Cataloguing in Publication Data

Sloan, Kathleen
    The global grill

Includes index.
ISBN 0-7788-0005-9

1. Barbecue cookery.   2. Cookery, International.   I. Title.

TX840.B3S56 1999   641.5'784   C99-930018-0

Photo Prop Credits

The publisher and author wish to express their appreciation to the following suppliers of props used in the food photography appearing in this book:

Dishes, cutlery, glassware, linens and accessories: **TABLE OF CONTENTS**
Queen's Quay Terminal, Toronto
(416) 203-1182

Barbecues: **WEBER - STEPHENS PRODUCTS CO.**
Manufacturer of Weber Barbecues

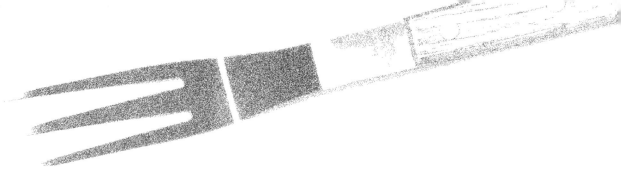

Dedication

This book is dedicated to the memory of my oldest friend, Marian Gayle Segee,whose search for beauty and truth in all things was lifelong.

Until we meet again, my friend,
... in Strawberry Fields Forever ...

Acknowledgements

First of all, a very appreciative thank you to Theresa Stahl and the generous people at Weber for introducing me to The Weber Performer Grill with Touch-N-Go Gas Ignition — an absolute honey of a charcoal grill, beautifully designed and complete with temperature gauge and every other conceivable "bell and whistle," which made me the envy of the neighborhood and all my friends who love to grill.

To Doug Boylin, a good buddy who proclaimed it "the easiest barbecue to assemble ever!" Thank you for all your help!

A heartfelt thank you to Bob Dees of Robert Rose, who allowed me to "internationalize" his original idea.

To Denise Schon with appreciation and thanks, once again.

To my friend — and grilling inspiration — Chef Ted Reader, who makes grilling a way of life! Thanks for giving everything your stamp of approval.

To food stylist Kate Bush for her enthusiasm and expertise — and for keeping me out of meetings so I could finish the book!

To Mark T. Shapiro for his beautiful photography…again! Thank you.

To Sharon Matthews for her creative work in making this one book that I hope everyone judges by the cover!

To Peter Matthews, and everyone at Matthews Communications Design, for being such a polished, pleasant and talented group of professionals.

To Mara Subotincic, warm thanks for all your work, helpful pointers and feedback.

To Nora Snikvalds, a willing and helpful home tester and taster, thanks once again!

Thank you too, to my daughter Jenna King for her deft way with desserts and sweets.

Introduction

Think globally…grill locally!

This is not a how-to book on grilling — it's a *what*-to! I'm willing to bet that if you've picked up this up book, you know something about grilling. After all, it's almost a seasonal national pastime. But I'm also willing to wager that you want to know more about *what* to grill. And I do mean grilling — not barbecuing. Real "barbecue" is another delicious creature altogether, as anyone from Texas, Kansas, Tennessee or South Carolina will be happy to point out. Simply stated, barbecuing describes the grilling of large, dense and economical joints of meat (beef or pork), that are cooked and smoked close to a slower heat for long periods of time to help them emerge crusty and moist. Anyone who has ever enjoyed traditional pulled pork in South Carolina or slow-smoked ribs in Tennessee will know precisely what real barbecue is. While these are bar-becued foods without peer, there is another world of grilling that involves less time and fuss, whose ingredients and style provide huge flavor and satisfaction, relying on a deck of international ingredients and cooking styles to give them their distinctive profiles.

So, this book is designed to introduce you to that world of great — and generally fast — grilling and fabulous eating, to rekindle your interest in cooking outside the kitchen door and to put an end forever to grill ennui.

From Korea's bulgogi to Australia's bush tucker cuisine, from South Africa's skewered sosaties to Southern Carolina's famous pulled pork sandwiches and Tuscany's juniper-scented spit-roasted chicken, it seems that every country and culture uses the grill or barbecue in one form or another to create traditional dishes that are unique to them alone.

The origins of barbecue are buried far back in time, with almost every cul-ture staking claim to the art of cooking with flame, smoke, wood and glowing coals. Some maintain the word "barbecue" derives from the French *barbe á queue* — "from beard to tail" — an apparent reference to the slow spit-roasting of a whole pig or cow over fire.

In Haiti and Guyana, Spanish conquistadors observed the Arawak Indians assembling their invention of a three-legged frame —dubbed a *barbacoa* — over great pits dug into the ground. Over these they would smoke fish and sear pork.

And so began the great barbecue begetting. From the Arawak, Caribbean and South American Indians to the Spanish. From the Spanish to the Greeks. From the Greeks to the Etruscans. From the Etruscans to the Romans. From the Romans to the English and on to the French, Chinese, Japanese, Moroccans, Brazilians, Portuguese, Burmese, Sri Lankans, Thai, East Indians, Vietnamese and, eventually, the North Americans.

Since as far back as 25 millennia, when open-flame pits were used to uphold massive carcasses, to today's sleek urban foolproof grills, capable of holding everything from cornish hens to seared scallops and portobello mushrooms, there has always been a primal and sensual appeal to the cooking of food outdoors.

From the Canadian foothills of Alberta and America's deep South, to the French region of Provence and Bangkok's street vendors, there is a whole world's worth of grilling to celebrate.

This is precisely the inspiration for *The Global Grill* and exactly what this book is all about: a celebration of international recipes, far beyond everyday fare, with contemporary appeal and flare, each of which enjoys a sizzling common denominator — the grill.

Whether you choose to use the rudimentary Japanese firebox called a hibachi, a modern gas grill, a covered kettle-style charcoal grill or an old iron rack set over bricks, these recipes, inspired by a barbecue and grill-loving world, will inject new life into everybody's favorite way to cook.

Kathleen Sloan

Getting Ready for the Global Grill

What do you need to grill on an "international" level? Not much more than you would for grilling everyday North American fare. Certainly the equipment is the same. The recipes in this book were tested on a Weber Performer Grill with Touch-N-Go Gas Ignition, as well as a conventional gas grill, with equally successful results.

Most of the recipes in this book were cooked over medium-high or high heat. Controlling heat on a gas grill is relatively easy, of course. But when using an everyday charcoal grill, you can easily check the heat levels by employing the "hand test": Hold the palm of your hand about 5 inches above the coals. If you can only bear it for 2 to 3 seconds, the fire is high; 3 to 4 seconds and the fire is medium-high; 4 to 6 seconds designates a fire of medium heat; while 7 to 9 seconds tells you the fire is relatively low.

My good friend Chef Ted Reader is a grilling expert without peer — and he maintains that whether you are planning to grill boneless chicken breasts, racks of ribs or a couple of fresh fish, there are three fundamentals rules for successful grilling:

- Make sure your fuel supply is sufficient;
- Make sure to always grease the grill before cooking; and
- Make sure to keep things moving on the grill to encourage even cooking

Sound advice, indeed. Now let me add a few of my own recommendations.

Get yourself organized before you prepare the grill. With quick-grill cooking, things happen pretty fast, so side dishes and accompanying sauces (among other things) should be tackled first — before you actually start grilling.

Ensure that food destined for the grill is cool but not refrigerator-cold. Bringing foods to room temperature before cooking means a shorter cooking time and more even cooking. Remember, too, that food continues to "cook" after it has been removed from the heat.

Keep the tongs and the spray bottle handy! Don't pierce meats unnecessarily; use tongs to turn and move foods around the grill. Extinguish little flare-ups with a couple of squirts from your spray bottle.

Grilling with International Flavors

Given the worldwide array of food styles currently in vogue, there's a good chance that you may already have most of the pantry staples called for in this book. Try to keep as many as possible on hand, as this will allow you to expand your culinary repertoire and provide a strong international accent to foods you grill. Information pertaining to many of the more unusual items appear next to the recipes in this book.

allspice, ground

almonds

annatto seeds

Asian fish sauce

bay leaves, fresh and dried

coconut milk and coconut cream, canned (look for light or low-fat)

cayenne pepper

cinnamon

coriander, fresh and dried

cumin

Dijon mustard

dry English mustard

fennel seed

five-spice powder

garlic

ginger root

ground ginger

herbes de Provence

hoisin sauce

hot Asian chili sauce

hot chili peppers, dried and fresh

lemon grass

lemons, oranges and limes

medium-dry sherry

mirin (Japanese rice wine)

oregano, fresh and dried (and Mexican oregano, dried)

nutmeg, whole

oil, olive and vegetable

paprika

peanuts

rosemary, dried and fresh

sake

sesame oil

shallots, onions, and green onions

soya sauce, light and dark varieties

thyme, fresh and dried

turmeric

vinegar: white and red wine, rice, balsamic and fruit vinegars such as raspberry and apple cider

Worcestershire sauce

Here are some of the other items that will assist in the preparation of recipes in this book:

Wooden skewers (use metal skewers when cooking times are longer)

Plastic containers with lids (or plastic bags with resealable closures) for marinating

A grill basket for grilling smaller items

A coffee mill for grinding spices

Long-handled cooking tongs

Basting brushes

A sturdy wire brush for cleaning the grill

Spray bottle

Meat thermometer

MARINADES, RUBS, PASTES, MOPPIN' SAUCES, GLAZES AND BUTTERS

MARINADES

Marmalade Mustard Marinade   15 • Citrus Trio Marinade   16
Masala Marinade   17 • Teriyaki Ginger Marinade   18
Polynesian Marinade   19 • Szechwan Marinade   20
Vietnamese Lemon Grass Marinade   21

RUBS

Mobay Jerk Rub   22 • Mexican Garlic Rub   23 • Five-Spice
Rub   24 • Santa Fe Red Chili Rub   25 • Provençal Rub   26
Tandoori-Style Rub   27

PASTES

Crimson Thai Paste   28 • Smoke and Fire Paste   29
Rosemary Lemon and Mustard Paste   30 • All-Round
Paste   31 • African Red Spice Paste   32

MOPPIN' SAUCES AND GLAZES

Double Bourbon Barbecue Sauce   33 • World's Greatest
Good-for-Everything Barbecue Sauce   34 • Mungo Mojo
Rojo   36 • Carolina Barbecue Sauce   37 • Peach Chutney
Glaze   38 • Pepper Pineapple and Rum Glaze   39

BUTTERS

Roquefort Butter   40 • Chive Parsley and Garlic Butter   41
Raspberry Mustard Butter   42 • Lavender Hill Butter   43
Salsa Butter   44 • Anchovy and Herb Butter   45 • Sun-
Dried Tomato and Oregano Butter   46 • Jalapeño Lemon
and Lime Butter   47 • Black Peppercorn and Garlic
Butter   48 • Tarragon and Shallot Butter   49 • Garlic and
Ginger Butter   50

Here is all you really need to know about marinades, spice pastes and sauces: they are designed to add flavor, pizzazz and, in some cases, to tenderize certain cuts of meat. A marinade can be as simple as a one-ingredient preparation such as a couple of steaks submerged in red wine before grilling. Generally speaking, however, a marinade will always contain an acid component (citrus, vinegar, wine), a fat (oil or butter) and an assortment of herbs and spices (garlic, freshly ground pepper, rosemary, etc.).

Sauces are used towards the latter half of cooking because they generally contain some form of sugar. Sauces enhance the flavor profile of what you're cooking.

Glazes are used at the very end of cooking or even after a food has left the grill.

Compound butters are a complement to food that is being served. Picture a hefty steak still sizzling and treated to a chunk of pungent Roquefort butter.

The more of these methods you employ, the bigger the payoff in terms of flavor intensity. Think of these preparations as support networks for grilling — the rules are more fast and loose than hard and fast, so get creative!

Marmalade Mustard Marinade

**Makes about
1 1/2 cups (375 mL)**

Because of marmalade's high sugar content, this recipe is best reserved for small items that require a short grilling time, such as a small chicken, shrimp, ham or pineapple on a skewer. This marinade may also be used as a glaze towards the end of grilling for boneless pork, chicken, duck or fish.

1/3 cup	orange or lemon marmalade	75 mL
1/4 cup	Dijon mustard	50 mL
1/3 cup	fresh orange juice	75 mL
1/4 cup	cider vinegar	50 mL
3 tbsp	vegetable oil	45 mL

1. In a bowl, blend marmalade and Dijon mustard. Whisk in orange juice, vinegar and vegetable oil.

2. Cover and refrigerate if not using immediately.

Citrus Trio Marinade

Makes about 1 cup (250 mL)

The best thing about this simple marinade is its versatility. Try it with chicken, pork, veal, fish steaks, shrimp or vegetables. Just remember that the acid in citrus acts as a tenderizer. Therefore, when using with chicken, pork or veal, marinate only up to 2 hours; with fish and seafood, no longer than 45 minutes.

To make it easier to extract all the juice from oranges, lemons and limes, place them in the microwave on High for 15 to 20 seconds before squeezing.

	Grated zest of 1 lemon	
1/4 cup	fresh lemon juice	50 mL
1/4 cup	fresh lime juice	50 mL
1/4 cup	fresh orange juice	50 mL
1/4 cup	extra virgin olive oil	50 mL
2	cloves garlic, minced	2
1 tsp	fennel seeds, crushed	5 mL
1/2 tsp	paprika	2 mL
1/2 tsp	salt	2 mL
1/4 tsp	freshly ground black pepper	1 mL

1. In a bowl whisk together lemon zest, lemon juice, lime juice, orange juice, olive oil, garlic, fennel seeds, paprika, salt and pepper.

2. Cover and refrigerate if not using immediately.

Masala Marinade

**Makes about 1 cup
(250 mL)**

A deeply flavorful marinade with a delightful East Indian accent, this will please all spice lovers. Make the garam masala ahead of time and store in a jar with a tight-fitting lid in a cool, dark, dry place.

Garam masala is an Indian preparation which translates as "hot spices." In India, the actual spices used vary with each household, but usually include cardamom, cloves, cumin, cinnamon and nutmeg.

Here is a classic garam masala combination that you can vary according to personal taste: 1 tbsp (15 mL) cardamom seeds, 1 tsp (5 mL) each of whole cloves, whole black peppercorns, whole mustard seeds and whole black cumin seeds (available at some specialty food shops and Indian food stores), a 2-inch (5 cm) stick of cinnamon and one-third of a whole nutmeg. Place all the ingredients in a coffee grinder and grind to a fine powder.

Without the wet ingredients, this mixture can be used as a dry rub for lamb, chicken, beef or pork.

6	cloves garlic, minced	6
1	shallot, minced	1
3 tbsp	fresh lemon juice	45 mL
3 tbsp	plain yogurt	45 mL
1 tbsp	chopped fresh coriander	15 mL
1 tbsp	chopped fresh mint	15 mL
1 to 2 tsp	garam masala (see notes at left)	5 to 10 mL
1 tsp	ground coriander	5 mL
1 tsp	ground cumin	5 mL
1 tsp	turmeric	5 mL
2/3 cup	vegetable oil	150 mL

1. In a bowl whisk together garlic, shallot, lemon juice, yogurt, fresh coriander, mint, garam masala, ground coriander, cumin and turmeric.

2. Add vegetable oil in a thin stream, whisking to blend well. Cover and refrigerate if not using immediately.

Teriyaki Ginger Marinade

Makes about 1 cup (250 mL)

Use this beautifully balanced marinade with boneless chicken breasts, salmon, tuna, swordfish steaks, shrimp, scallops or brushed over portobello mushrooms.

This mixture may also be used as a post-grill glaze on all of the above foods by cooking it in a small saucepan over medium heat until thickened and somewhat reduced. Brush over food while still on the grill.

Mirin is a low-alcohol sweet wine made from rice and is available at Japanese markets, some specialty food shops and often in the international section of many supermarkets.

A garlic press is the perfect tool with which to extract fresh ginger juice. Simply peel the ginger, cut into small pieces and fit in the press. Squeeze over a bowl to catch the juice.

1/3 cup	*mirin* (sweet rice wine)	75 mL
1/3 cup	*sake* (rice wine)	75 mL
1/3 cup	tamari (Japanese soya sauce)	75 mL
1 tbsp	light brown sugar	15 mL
1	clove garlic, finely minced	1
	Juice of 1 piece ginger root (see note, lower left, for technique)	

1. In a small mixing bowl, blend *mirin*, *sake* and tamari. Whisk in brown sugar, garlic and ginger juice.

2. Cover and refrigerate if not using immediately.

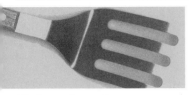

Polynesian Marinade

**Makes about 1 cup
(250 mL)**

This flavorful marinade is one of my favorites. Adjust the amount of hot chili sauce according to taste.

In this recipe, light soya sauce is not "lite" soya sauce. It refers rather to the product's color and density. Look for light soya sauce in Chinese groceries or specialty food shops. It is quite different from regular soya sauce.

Chinese fermented black beans are often sold as preserved black beans.

2 tbsp	Chinese fermented black beans	25 mL
1/4 cup	hoisin sauce	50 mL
1/4 cup	pineapple juice	50 mL
3 tbsp	light soya sauce	45 mL
3 tbsp	rice wine vinegar	45 mL
2 tbsp	honey	25 mL
2 tbsp	sesame oil	25 mL
1 tbsp	hot chili sauce	15 mL
1	clove garlic, minced	1
	Grated zest of 1 orange	

1. Rinse black beans under hot water. Drain; pat dry with a paper towel. Transfer beans to a bowl. Using the back of a fork, press beans against sides of bowl until fairly well mashed.

2. Add hoisin sauce, pineapple juice, soya sauce, vinegar, honey, sesame oil, chili sauce, garlic and orange zest; blend together well. Cover and refrigerate if not using immediately.

Szechwan Marinade

Makes about 1 cup (250 mL)

Chinese five-spice powder gives this fragrant marinade its spicy sweetness which is balanced with a little heat from hot chili oil. This marinade can also be used as a brushing sauce. With its pronounced anise flavor, it is especially good with fish. Use also with beef, chicken and duck.

The ancient formula for five-spice powder included star anise, Szechwan peppercorns, cinnamon, clove and fennel. One explanation for the name stems from the Chinese belief that the universe is made up of five elements — wood, metal, water, fire and earth — elements that must be carefully balanced to provide harmony. Five-spice powder originally was attributed with powerful medicinal properties.

Look for five-spice powder in Chinese supermarkets, Asian specialty shops and the dried spice or international section of large supermarkets. Alternatively, make your own five-spice powder (see recipe for FIVE-SPICE RUB, page 24).

2	green onions, finely minced	2
1/4 cup	minced fresh chives	50 mL
1/4 cup	soya sauce	50 mL
1/4 cup	*sake* (Japanese rice wine) or pale dry sherry	50 mL
2 tbsp	minced ginger root	25 mL
2 tbsp	sesame oil	25 mL
2 tbsp	Chinese red chili oil	25 mL
2 tsp	five-spice powder	10 mL

1. In a bowl whisk together green onions, chives, soya sauce, *sake*, ginger, sesame oil, chili and five-spice powder.

2. Cover and refrigerate if not using immediately.

Vietnamese Lemon Grass Marinade

**Makes about
1 1/2 cups (375 mL)**

Magnificent lemon grass is the definitive ingredient in Southeast Asian cooking. In Thailand, it is used in soups, curries and salads, while the Vietnamese often choose it as the basis for their tangy marinades. In my opinion, lemon grass provides a more soothing citrus influence than lemons — just as effective but less "loud" overall. This adaptable preparation lends much intense flavor to chicken and seafood, but I also like it as a marinade for flank steak.

When buying lemon grass, look for firm stalks with a nice-sized bulb. When fresh it should be firm with a pale- to light-green hue and a bulb of palest pink. Pass over any that are dry and yellowed. Before chopping, peel away the tough outer layer of the stalk and trim the root end. To make the stalks easier to chop finely, slice them (as you would a green onion) into thin rounds, removing any long fibrous bits as you work. This process may be done in a food processor if you plan on chopping a great deal of lemon grass.

1/4 cup	chopped lemon grass stalks	50 mL
2 tbsp	packed light brown sugar	25 mL
3	cloves garlic, minced	3
2	shallots, minced	2
1 or 2	red Thai chilies, seeded and minced	1 or 2
1/4 cup	vegetable oil	50 mL
	Juice of 3 limes	
3 tbsp	Asian fish sauce	45 mL
3 tbsp	rice vinegar	45 mL
1 tbsp	hot chili sauce	15 mL

1. In a bowl combine lemon grass, brown sugar, garlic, shallots and chilies. Using the back of a large spoon, work ingredients together to form a chunky paste.

2. Gradually add vegetable oil, pressing and mashing with the back of a spoon. Stir in lime juice, fish sauce, rice vinegar and chili sauce. Blend together well.

3. Cover and refrigerate if not using immediately.

Mobay Jerk Rub

**Makes about
2/3 cup (150 mL)**

Because dry rubs have no oil or acid components, they are perhaps the most flavorful of all the pregrilling treatments. This particular one is inspired by Jamaica's famous jerk seasoning mixture and, while not completely traditional, packs a seriously good spice island punch. If you prefer a "wet" jerk marinade or paste, try JAMAICAN JERK PORK (see recipe, page 106).

2 tbsp	allspice	25 mL
2 tbsp	minced fresh thyme	25 mL
2 tbsp	packed dark brown sugar	25 mL
1 tbsp	cinnamon	15 mL
1 tbsp	paprika	15 mL
2 tsp	freshly grated nutmeg	10 mL
2 tsp	ground ginger	10 mL
2 tsp	ground red pepper	10 mL
1 tsp	dried thyme leaves	5 mL
1 tsp	ground habanero pepper	5 mL
1 tsp	salt	5 mL
1 tsp	freshly ground black pepper	5 mL

1. In a bowl stir together allspice, fresh thyme, brown sugar, cinnamon, paprika, nutmeg, ginger, red pepper, dried thyme, habanero pepper, salt and pepper. Store in a jar with a tight-fitting lid.

Mexican Garlic Rub

**Makes about
3/4 cup (175 mL)**

You will need a coffee grinder or spice mill for this recipe.

Mexican oregano is a much stronger flavored herb than conventional oregano. Look for it in Mexican or Latin American supermarkets.

This rub is wonderful with legs of lamb, a hefty steak, lobster tails, shrimp or chicken.

Preheat oven to 150° F (65° C)
Baking sheet, nonstick or greased

2 tbsp	dried Mexican oregano	25 mL
2 tbsp	cumin seeds, toasted	25 mL
8	whole allspice berries	8
3	whole cloves	3
1	head garlic, oven-roasted until soft	1
1/4 cup	chopped fresh coriander	50 mL
1/4 cup	chopped fresh mint	50 mL
2 tbsp	coarse salt	25 mL
1 tbsp	freshly ground black pepper	15 mL

1. In a spice mill or clean coffee grinder, grind together oregano, cumin, allspice and cloves to a fine powder.

2. When garlic is cool enough to handle, peel at least 10 cloves.

3. In a food processor, combine ground spices and garlic. Add coriander, mint, salt and pepper. Pulse on and off until mixture is coarse and crumbly.

4. Spread mixture (which should be a little damp) onto baking sheet. Bake in preheated oven, stirring occasionally for 1 hour or until completely dry.

5. Store in a jar with a tight-fitting lid at room temperature.

Five-Spice Rub

**Makes about
1/2 cup (125 mL)**

Making your own five-spice powder results in a wonderfully fresh-tasting, ultra-fragrant rub. Be careful to use judiciously or it can be overpowering. Rub into whole chickens, duck breasts, pork tenderloins, lamb sausages or lamb chops.

Star anise is a pretty, star-shaped dark brown pod with eight segments, each of which contain a seed. A member of the magnolia family, star anise is the most important component of five-spice powder and is responsible for its characteristic flavor. Look for it in Asian markets and in the spice section of larger supermarkets.

Szechwan peppercorns are often labeled as dried red pepper in Asian markets. They are not really peppercorns at all, in the strict sense of the word, but dried berries that contain a tiny seed. They come from the Chinese prickly ash tree.

12	star anise pods	12
2 tbsp	fennel seeds	25 mL
2 tbsp	Szechwan peppercorns	25 mL
1 tbsp	whole cloves	15 mL
1	4-inch (10 cm) cinnamon stick, broken into pieces	1

1. In a spice mill or clean coffee grinder, combine star anise, fennel, peppercorns, cloves and cinnamon. Grind to a fine powder.

2. Store in a jar with a tight-fitting lid at room temperature.

Santa Fe Red Chili Rub

**Makes about
1/2 cup (125 mL)**

This is a no-nonsense rub, tailor-made for big steaks. Make sure to allow this dry rub to sit on the meat for at least 30 minutes to allow the beef to absorb the flavors. Team rubbed steaks with a bold, smoky barbecue sauce for maximum effect.

Look to specialty food shops or Mexican and Latin American markets for varieties of ground red chili powders (never to be confused with the ubiquitous, mild-mannered and rather ineffective chili powder blends used to make substandard chili con carne). Chipotle (smoke-dried jalapeño), *guajillo* (or Anaheim) and ancho chili powders (or a mixture) would be good choices for this recipe. While all have some heat, they are not the hottest available — an important consideration, since your choice will be teamed with hot red pepper flakes.

1/4 cup	hot red pepper flakes	50 mL
1/4 cup	red chili powder	50 mL
1 tbsp	dried oregano	15 mL
1 tsp	granulated sugar	5 mL
1/2 tsp	salt	2 mL
1/2 tsp	freshly ground black pepper	2 mL

1. In a skillet (preferably cast iron) over medium heat, toast hot red pepper flakes, chili powder and oregano, stirring and occasionally shaking pan, for 2 minutes or until spices are fragrant. Remove from heat; cool slightly. Pour into a spice grinder or clean coffee grinder; grind to a fine powder.

2. In a bowl stir together ground spice mixture, sugar, salt and pepper. Store in a jar with a tight-fitting lid at room temperature.

Provençal Rub

**Makes about
1/2 cup (125 mL)**

While ready-made dried mixtures of *herbes de Provence* are widely available, try this combination at least once — it's delicious on lamb destined for the grill.

2 tbsp	dried thyme leaves	25 mL
1 tbsp	dried basil	15 mL
1 tbsp	dried marjoram	15 mL
1 tbsp	dried rosemary leaves	15 mL
2 tsp	dried summer savory	10 mL
1 tsp	fennel seeds	5 mL
1 tsp	dried lavender flowers	5 mL

1. In a bowl, combine thyme, basil, marjoram, rosemary, savory, fennel seeds and lavender. With your hands, crush and mix herbs until well blended. (For a finer blend, grind in a spice grinder or a clean coffee grinder.)

2. Store in a jar with a tight-fitting lid at room temperature.

Tandoori-Style Rub

**Makes about
1/3 cup (75 mL)**

This Indian-influenced rub will simply transform chicken, cornish hens, shrimp and fish headed for the grill. Serve tandoori-rubbed meats or fish with a fragrant basmati rice pilau and a cooling side dish such as LEBANESE CUCUMBER AND MINT SALAD (see recipe, page 174).

2 tsp	ground coriander	10 mL
2 tsp	ground cumin	10 mL
2 tsp	garam masala (see MASALA MARINADE, page 17)	10 mL
2 tsp	ground ginger	10 mL
2 tsp	paprika	10 mL
2 tsp	turmeric	10 mL
1 tsp	ground cardamom	5 mL
1 tsp	salt	5 mL
1 tsp	ground white pepper	5 mL
1/2 tsp	cayenne	2 mL
4	cloves garlic, finely minced	4

1. In a bowl stir together coriander, cumin, garam masala, ginger, paprika, turmeric, cardamom, salt, white pepper and cayenne. Store in a jar with a tight-fitting lid at room temperature.

2. When ready to grill, add garlic to mixture. Rub onto meat.

Crimson Thai Paste

**Makes about
1 1/2 cups (375 mL)**

This Thai-influenced paste is vibrant in color and flavor, highlighted by the pungency of fresh chilies. Wonderful as a wet rub for tiger shrimp or boneless chicken breasts, it is also excellent with pork tenderloin, swordfish steaks or squid.

When working with fresh chilies, wear rubber gloves to protect your skin from the fiery qualities in the chili's seeds and oil. Also, keep your hands away from your face — especially your eyes. Plain yogurt is a good, soothing antidote for a chili burn — internally and externally!

Smear paste onto chicken or meat about 15 minutes before grilling. If using with shrimp or fish, apply just before grilling.

1 tbsp	coriander seeds	15 mL
2 tsp	cumin seeds	10 mL
4	small fresh red chilies	4
6	cloves garlic	6
4	stalks lemon grass, trimmed and finely chopped (for technique, see page 21)	4
1	white onion, quartered	1
1/3 cup	canned unsweetened coconut milk	75 mL
3 tbsp	minced ginger root	45 mL
1 tbsp	paprika	15 mL
	Grated zest and juice of 1 lemon	
	Grated zest and juice of 1 lime	

1. In a small heavy skillet over medium heat, toast coriander and cumin seeds, shaking skillet and stirring, for 2 minutes or until fragrant. Remove from heat. Cool slightly. In a spice grinder or clean coffee grinder, grind to a fine powder.

2. In a food processor, combine ground spice mixture, chilies, garlic, lemon grass, onion, coconut milk, ginger, paprika, lemon zest, lemon juice, lime zest and lime juice. Using on/off button, process to a paste, adding a little more coconut milk if needed. Store in refrigerator or freezer.

Smoke and Fire Paste

**Makes about
1 cup (250 mL)**

This is an extremely simple-to-prepare paste that relies on the wonderfully powerful quality of chipotles to work its magic. Chipotles are smoked jalapeños and, when canned, are packed in a rich, lustrous tomato and onion sauce called adobo. The smokiness of chipotle peppers in adobo sauce makes this paste a natural choice for ribs, pork and burgers. You won't need a great deal of this to coat chicken or meat, so store the remainder, covered, in the refrigerator.

For those who would like a little less fire in this paste, deseed the chipotles, wearing rubber gloves, by slitting them open and scraping away the seeds and membrane with the side of a paring knife.

8	canned chipotles, finely chopped	8
3 tbsp	adobo sauce (from canned chipotles)	45 mL
1/2 cup	frozen lemonade concentrate, thawed	125 mL
1/4 cup	chopped fresh coriander	50 mL
	Grated zest of 1 lemon	

1. In a food processor, combine chipotles, adobo sauce, lemonade, coriander and lemon zest. Using on/off button, process to a smooth paste. Store covered in refrigerator.

Rosemary Lemon and Mustard Paste

**Makes about
1 cup (250 mL)**

Here's the perfect paste for a boneless butterflied leg of lamb. While you may find it a little moister than the others, this in no way detracts from its qualities. This paste also works well with chicken and pork.

Try adding a small amount of the PROVENÇAL RUB (see recipe, page 26) to this paste.

3 tbsp	honey	45 mL
3 tbsp	Dijon mustard	45 mL
3 tbsp	olive oil	45 mL
3 tbsp	chopped fresh rosemary	45 mL
4	cloves garlic, minced	4
3	shallots, minced	3
	Grated zest and juice of 1 lemon	
1 tsp	salt	5 mL
1/2 tsp	freshly ground black pepper	2 mL

1. In a bowl stir together honey, mustard, olive oil, rosemary, garlic, shallots, lemon zest, lemon juice, salt and pepper.

2. Smear onto meat or chicken; let stand for 15 minutes before grilling. If using with seafood, apply just before grilling.

All-Round Paste

**Makes about
1 1/4 cups (300 mL)**

Not exotic in the least, this is a straightforward paste that works well with beef, pork, burgers, chicken and just about anything else you can grill.

1	large onion, cut into chunks	1
4	cloves garlic	4
2 tbsp	dry mustard	25 mL
2 tbsp	packed light brown sugar	25 mL
1 tsp	salt	5 mL
1 tsp	freshly ground black pepper	5 mL
1 tsp	paprika	5 mL
1/4 cup	olive oil	50 mL
3 tbsp	red wine	45 mL
3 tbsp	Worcestershire sauce	45 mL

1. In a food processor, combine onion, garlic, mustard, brown sugar, salt, pepper, paprika, olive oil, red wine and Worcestershire sauce. Using on/off button, process to a paste. Store covered in refrigerator.

African Red Spice Paste

**Makes about
2 cups (500 mL)**

Traditionally paired with raw chopped beef, this fiery concoction is called *berberé* in Ethiopia. Use with discretion to coat beef, chicken, pork and shellfish. Store remaining paste, covered, in the refrigerator.

1 tsp	ground ginger	5 mL
1/2 tsp	ground cardamom	2 mL
1/2 tsp	ground coriander	2 mL
1/2 tsp	freshly grated nutmeg	2 mL
1/4 tsp	ground cloves	1 mL
1/4 tsp	ground cinnamon	1 mL
1/4 tsp	ground allspice	1 mL
1	white onion, cut into chunks	1
3	cloves garlic, peeled	3
3 tbsp	red wine vinegar	45 mL
2 tsp	salt	10 mL
1 cup	paprika	250 mL
1 tbsp	cayenne	15 mL
1 tsp	freshly ground black pepper	5 mL
3/4 to 1 cup	water	175 to 250 mL
1 tbsp	vegetable oil	15 mL

1. In a large heavy skillet or Dutch oven, toast ginger, cardamom, coriander, nutmeg, cloves, cinnamon and allspice over low heat, stirring constantly and shaking pan back and forth occasionally, for 2 minutes, or until spices become fragrant. Remove from heat; cool slightly.

2. In a food processor or blender, combine toasted spices with onion, garlic, vinegar and 1 tsp (5 mL) salt. Process until mixture becomes paste-like.

3. In the same heavy skillet, combine paprika, cayenne, black pepper and remaining salt; toast spices over medium heat, stirring continually and shaking pan, or for 3 minutes until fragrant.

Recipe continues next page...

CHILLED GRILLED RED PEPPER SOUP WITH CRÈME FRAÎCHE (PAGE 53) ➤

4. Remove from heat; cool slightly. Scrape into a clean, dry jar, pressing with the back of a spoon to pack in. If not using right away (or for leftover paste), when mixture is completely cool, pour a little vegetable oil over surface. Cover and refrigerate.

◄ GRILLED PIZZA WITH PANCETTA, PORCINI AND FONTINA (PAGE 61)

World's Greatest Good-for-Everything Barbecue Sauce

**Makes about
3 cups (750 mL)**

There are dozens of very good commercially prepared barbecue sauces on the market. Some are smoky, some sweet, some have a tang and some pack heat. If you are passionate about one in particular, by all means use it. But when you're in the mood to whip up one of your own, choose this recipe — it produces a sauce that seems to improve everything it touches, although it's at its best with chicken, pork and slabs of ribs.

Heat-seekers may want to add their favorite hot component to this sauce. Choose either fresh chopped chilies, hot sauce, cayenne or red pepper flakes. If using fresh chilies, add them along with the onion and garlic; hot sauce can be included along with the wet ingredients, while the cayenne, red pepper flakes or any other spices may be added along with the dry.

1 tbsp	vegetable oil	15 mL
1	white onion, chopped	1
3	cloves garlic, minced	3
1 cup	canned puréed tomatoes	250 mL
3/4 cup	apple cider vinegar	175 mL
3/4 cup	beef stock	175 mL
1/4 cup	ketchup	50 mL
3 tbsp	tomato paste	45 mL
1/4 cup	Worcestershire sauce	50 mL
2 tsp	horseradish	10 mL
1/4 cup	packed dark brown sugar	50 mL
3 tbsp	chili powder	45 mL
2 tsp	dry English mustard	10 mL
1 tbsp	paprika	15 mL
2 tsp	salt	10 mL
1 tbsp	freshly ground black pepper	15 mL
1 tsp	cinnamon	5 mL

1. In a heavy saucepan, warm oil over medium heat. Add onion and garlic; cook for 5 minutes or until pale gold and softened.

2. Add tomatoes, vinegar, stock, ketchup, tomato paste, Worcestershire sauce and horseradish; stir to blend well.

3. Using a whisk, blend in sugar, chili powder, mustard, paprika, salt, pepper and cinnamon. Bring to a boil. Reduce heat; cook, stirring occasionally, for 25 to 30 minutes or until thickened and sauce-like. (If mixture is thicker than you like, add a little additional stock or water.)

4. Use sauce during last 15 minutes of grilling. Set some sauce aside (untouched by basting brush) to serve tableside. Or, pour remaining sauce into a saucepan; boil for 3 minutes.

Double Bourbon Barbecue Sauce

**Makes about
2 3/4 cups (675 mL)**

Absolutely fantastic with chicken, this is my all-time favorite barbecue sauce. Versatile and packed with the favorite flavors of the old South, you can also use the sauce as a marinade. If you choose to use it this way, be sure to pour the remaining sauce into a small saucepan and bring to a boil for about 3 minutes before using as a barbecue or mopping sauce.

Try also with beef ribs or pork.

2 tbsp	vegetable oil	25 mL
1	onion, chopped	1
3	cloves garlic, minced	3
1 tbsp	freshly grated orange zest	15 mL
1/2 cup	freshly squeezed orange juice	125 mL
1/4 cup	chopped fresh mint	50 mL
2 tbsp	balsamic vinegar	25 ml
1/2 cup	bourbon whiskey	125 mL
1/3 cup	molasses	75 mL
1/4 cup	Dijon mustard (or other mustard)	50 mL
1/2 cup	ketchup	125 mL
1 tbsp	Worcestershire sauce	15 mL
1/4 tsp	salt	1 mL
1/4 tsp	freshly ground black pepper	1 mL

1. In a bowl, combine oil, onion, garlic, orange zest, orange juice, mint, vinegar, bourbon, molasses, mustard, ketchup, Worcestershire sauce, salt and pepper.

2. Store covered in refrigerator.

Mungo Mojo Rojo

**Makes
2 cups (500 mL)**

A Mojo is a type of sauce or condiment that Cubans use with the sort of abandon that North Americans reserve for ketchup and, more recently, salsa. It makes an excellent marinade, a superb basting mixture and a typically Cuban sauce for barbecuing. Don't let the fact that it is a bit thinner than traditional barbecue sauces fool you into thinking it has a mild-mannered temperament — it is Cuban, after all!

In Cuba, sour oranges (like Bittersweet or Seville varieties) would be used in place of the lime juice in this mojo. If they are available, by all means use them.

This sauce will keep up to 3 weeks, covered and refrigerated.

6	cloves garlic, minced	6
1	fresh chili (habanero or Thai), seeded and minced	1
2 tsp	cumin seeds, toasted	10 mL
1 tsp	dried oregano	5 mL
1/2 tsp	salt	2 mL
1/3 cup	freshly squeezed lime juice	75 mL
2	red bell peppers, grilled, seeded and peeled	2
1/2 cup	vegetable oil	125 mL
2 tbsp	red wine vinegar	25 mL
1/2 tsp	freshly ground black pepper	2 mL

1. Wearing rubber gloves, arrange garlic, chili, cumin, oregano and salt on a cutting board. Using a sharp chef's knife, finely mince.

2. Scrape mixture into a food processor or blender. Add lime juice, peppers, oil, vinegar and pepper. Using on/off button, purée until mixture is smooth.

3. Store covered in refrigerator.

Carolina Barbecue Sauce

**Makes
2 cups (500 mL)**

Authentic barbecue in Carolina means pork and nothing "butt"! And that typically slow-cooked pork demands the sharp, clean taste of this intentionally thin, vinegar-based barbecue sauce.

2 cups	apple cider vinegar	500 mL
1/4 cup	packed dark brown sugar	50 mL
2 tbsp	hot sauce	25 mL
2 tsp	salt	10 mL
1 tsp	freshly ground black pepper	5 mL

1. In a small saucepan over medium heat, combine vinegar and brown sugar, stirring until sugar is dissolved.

2. Add hot sauce, salt and pepper. Cook, stirring, for 5 minutes; sauce will be thin. Use half as a marinade, half as a basting mop.

Peach Chutney Glaze

**Makes
2 cups (500 mL)**

Treat grilled ham steaks, ribs or pork chops to this fruity, spicy glaze. It is best used towards the last 10 minutes of grilling.

Look for good quality peach chutney for this recipe.

1 cup	peach chutney	250 mL
1/2 cup	whiskey	125 mL
1/3 cup	white wine vinegar	75 mL
3 tbsp	Worcestershire sauce	45 mL
1/2 tsp	freshly grated nutmeg	2 mL
1/4 tsp	ground allspice	1 mL
1/2 tsp	ground cinnamon	2 mL
1 tsp	curry powder	5 mL
	Juice of 1 lemon	

1. In a small heavy-bottomed saucepan over medium heat, combine peach chutney, whiskey, vinegar, Worcestershire sauce, nutmeg, allspice, cinnamon and curry. Stir; bring mixture to a simmer.

2. Reduce heat to medium-low; cook for 10 minutes or until slightly thickened. Stir in lemon juice. Make sure sauce is hot when applied.

3. Store covered in refrigerator.

Pepper, Pineapple and Rum Glaze

**Makes about
1 1/2 cups (375 mL)**

Sweet and hot — perfect for boneless chicken breasts, fish steaks, shrimp or pork.

1 cup	red pepper jelly	250 mL
1/4 cup	light rum	50 mL
1/4 cup	pineapple juice	50 mL
1/4 cup	chopped fresh mint	50 mL
1	habanero (or Thai) chili, seeded and minced	1

1. In a small heavy-bottomed saucepan over medium-low heat, warm jelly, rum and pineapple juice. Stir until jelly is melted.

2. Remove pan from heat; add mint and chili. Let sauce stand for 30 minutes, allowing flavors to develop. Use during last 10 minutes of grilling. Make sure glaze is hot when applied.

Roquefort Butter

**Makes
3/4 cup (175 mL)**

1/2 cup	Roquefort cheese, crumbled and mashed with a fork	125 mL
1/2 cup	softened butter	125 mL

1. In a bowl combine cheese and butter. Cream ingredients together until well blended. Follow directions at left for wrapping and chilling.

Butters

All of these prepared butters enhance steaks, chicken, burgers, baked potatoes, fresh corn, grilled vegetables and pasta salads. Use your imagination and combine fresh herbs with your favorite cheeses or condiments.

The easiest and fastest way to make any of these savory butters is with a food processor. However, I prefer to make them by hand as I have a little more control over the blending and final consistency of the butter. It is not at all difficult and rather satisfying. Use a metal or rubber spatula or the back of a spoon to work the butter and other ingredients together to form a creamy paste.

To form the butter into a nice log shape — which in turn will result in neat, coin-shaped pieces of butter once it has been chilled — lay out a piece of plastic wrap on a clean, dry surface. Using a rubber spatula, arrange the butter along the length of the wrap to form a log. Partially cover with half of the wrap and roll back and forth with your hands until it begins to take the shape of a log. Wrap tightly at both ends and refrigerate until well chilled. Butters will keep for about a week in the refrigerator.

Chive Parsley and Garlic Butter

**Makes
1/2 cup (125 mL)**

Wonderful with grilled porter-house steaks or lamb chops. Use more or less garlic according to taste.

2	cloves garlic, minced	2
2 tbsp	chopped fresh parsley	25 mL
2 tbsp	chopped fresh chives	25 mL
1 tsp	Worcestershire sauce	5 mL
1/2 cup	softened butter	125 mL
	Salt and freshly ground black pepper, to taste	

1. In a bowl, combine garlic, parsley, chives, Worcestershire sauce and butter. Cream together until well blended. Season to taste with salt and pepper. Follow directions on page 40 for wrapping and chilling.

Raspberry Mustard Butter

**Makes
3/4 cup (175 mL)**

This is outstanding with grilled fish, shrimp, duck or pork.

1/2 cup	chopped fresh raspberries	125 mL
1 tbsp	Dijon mustard	15 mL
1 tbsp	raspberry vinegar	15 mL
1/2 cup	softened butter	125 mL
	Salt and freshly ground black pepper, to taste	

1. In a bowl combine raspberries, mustard, vinegar and butter. Cream together until well blended. Season to taste with salt and pepper. Follow directions on page 40 for wrapping and chilling.

Lavender Hill Butter

Makes
1/2 cup (125 mL)

Strongly reminiscent of the flavors of Provence, this is the best butter for lamb. Be sure to choose the freshest (preferably organic) lavender for this recipe; otherwise it will prove to be too strong. If you can find lavender honey for this recipe, so much the better.

2	shallots, minced	2
2 tbsp	Champagne or white wine vinegar	25 mL
2 tbsp	honey	25 mL
1/2 cup	softened butter	125 mL
2 to 4	fresh lavender flower heads, minced (or 1 tsp [5 mL] dried lavender flowers)	2 to 4
	Salt and freshly ground white pepper, to taste	

1. In a bowl combine shallots, Champagne, honey, butter and lavender flowers. Cream together until well blended. Season to taste with salt and pepper. Follow directions on page 40 for wrapping and chilling.

Salsa Butter

Makes
3/4 cup (175 mL)

Use your favorite brand of salsa for this recipe or make your own. For a great variation on the theme here, add cubes of ripe avocado along with the salsa or substitute guacamole for the salsa entirely. Good with just about everything, this butter is wonderful with chicken, fish or vegetarian burgers.

1/4 cup	salsa	50 mL
2 tbsp	chopped fresh coriander	25 mL
1/2 cup	softened butter	125 mL

1. In a bowl combine salsa, coriander and butter. Cream together until well blended. Follow directions on page 40 for wrapping and chilling.

Anchovy and Herb Butter

**Makes
1/2 cup (125 mL)**

This butter is very good with mild-tasting meats like veal or pork. Melted, it makes a great flavor booster when brushed over flatbreads and pizzas before adding toppings.

1 tsp	tomato paste	5 mL
1	large clove garlic, minced	1
4	anchovy fillets, drained and minced	4
1/2 tsp	*herbes de Provence*, crumbled	2 mL
1/2 tsp	paprika	2 mL
1/2 cup	softened butter	125 mL
1/4 tsp	freshly ground black pepper	1 mL

1. In a bowl combine tomato paste, garlic, anchovy fillets, *herbes de Provence*, paprika, butter and pepper. Cream together until well blended. Follow directions on page 40 for wrapping and chilling.

Sun-Dried Tomato and Oregano Butter

**Makes
2/3 cup (150 mL)**

This Italian-influenced butter is colorful and pretty. Try it with hefty grilled veal chops or melting into mashed potatoes.

4	cloves garlic, minced	4
1/2 cup	softened butter	125 mL
6	sun-dried tomatoes, packed in oil, drained and minced	6
3 tbsp	chopped fresh oregano	45 mL
1/4 tsp	freshly ground black pepper	1 mL
	Salt	

1. In a bowl combine garlic, butter, sun-dried tomatoes, oregano and pepper. Cream together until well blended. Season to taste with salt. Follow directions on page 40 for wrapping and chilling.

Jalapeño Lemon and Lime Butter

**Makes
2/3 cup (150 mL)**

A natural choice for any grilled seafood — especially lobster and shrimp — this butter is also great with chicken and grilled vegetables such as corn-on-the-cob or an assortment of charred peppers.

Adjust the amount of jalapeño to your taste. Remember to use rubber gloves when handling fresh chilies and avoid all contact with your face.

2	jalapeños, trimmed, seeded and minced	2
1 tbsp	finely grated lemon zest	15 mL
2 tbsp	finely grated lime zest	25 mL
2 tbsp	chopped fresh coriander	25 mL
1/2 cup	softened butter	125 mL
1/4 tsp	freshly ground black pepper	1 mL
	Salt	

1. In a bowl combine jalapeños, lemon zest, lime zest, coriander, butter and pepper. Cream together until well blended. Season to taste with salt. Follow directions on page 40 for wrapping and chilling.

Black Peppercorn and Garlic Butter

**Makes
2/3 cup (150 mL)**

In this classic combination, try varying the color of the peppercorns from time to time, using pink, green, white or black. Adjust your peppermill to grind the peppercorns coarsely or crush them using a mortar and pestle.

1 tbsp	black peppercorns, coarsely ground	15 mL
3	shallots, minced	3
1	large clove garlic, minced	1
1/2 cup	softened butter	125 mL
	Salt	

1. In a bowl, combine peppercorns, shallots, garlic and butter. Cream together until well blended. Season to taste with salt. Follow directions on page 40 for wrapping and chilling.

Tarragon and Shallot Butter

**Makes
3/4 cup (175 mL)**

Great with fish, shellfish,
lamb and chicken.

2 tbsp	chopped fresh tarragon	25 mL
2 tbsp	chopped fresh parsley	25 mL
2	shallots, minced	2
2 tbsp	finely grated lemon zest	25 mL
	Juice of half a lemon	
1/2 cup	softened butter	125 mL
	Salt and freshly ground black pepper, to taste	

1. In a bowl combine tarragon, parsley, shallots, lemon zest, lemon juice and butter. Cream together until well blended. Season to taste with salt and pepper. Follow directions on page 40 for wrapping and chilling.

Garlic and Ginger Butter

Makes
1/2 cup (125 mL)

Lovely with grilled pork
chops, shrimps, scallops,
chicken and vegetables.

1	large clove garlic, minced	1
2 tsp	grated ginger root	10 mL
1/2 cup	softened butter	125 mL
	Freshly ground black pepper, to taste	

1. In a bowl combine garlic, ginger and butter. Cream
   together until well blended. Season to taste with pepper.
   Follow directions on page 40 for wrapping and chilling.

COOL SOUPS & STARTERS

SOUPS
Cucumber Soup with Mint and Chive   52
Chilled Grilled Red Pepper Soup with Crème Fraîche   53
Grilled Corn Soup with Pesto Swirl   54
Cream of Watercress Soup with Nasturtiums   56
Cool Tomato Soup with Basil and Mint Toasts   58
Tortilla and Lime Soup Zocalo   60

STARTERS
Grilled Pizza with Pancetta, Porcini and Fontina   61
Asian-Flavored Tuna with Cucumber   62
Spanish Shrimp   63
Grilled Polenta   64
Grilled Lamb on Lavosh   65
Singapore Satay   66
Julia's Potato and Jalapeño Quesadillas   68
Grilled Bacon and Zucchini Wrapped Scallops   69
Southeast Asian Dumplings   70
Spanish Meatballs in Salsa Roja   72
Yakitori   74
Royal Thai Wings   75
Late Summer Vegetable and Chèvre Terrine   76
Grilled Peppers with Cheese   78
Smoked Trout Spread   79

Cucumber Soup with Mint and Chive

Serves 4 to 6

Every once in a while, during the heat of summer, you'll experience an insatiable craving for the coolness of this creamy cucumber soup. The refreshing addition of fresh mint and chives elevates all the flavors immeasurably. This soup is wonderful as an elegant precursor to a spicy grilled main dish.

1/2 cup	sour cream	125 mL
1/2 cup	plain yogurt	125 mL
1 cup	buttermilk	250 mL
1/4 cup	fresh lime juice	50 mL
1/2 cup	packed fresh mint leaves	125 mL
2	English cucumbers halved lengthwise, seeded and coarsely chopped	2
1/4 cup	chopped fresh chives	50 mL
Pinch	cayenne	Pinch
	Salt and freshly ground white pepper, to taste	

1. In a blender or food processor, combine sour cream, yogurt, buttermilk, lime juice and mint; process until combined. Add chopped cucumbers 1 cup (250 mL) at a time, processing until smooth after each addition.

2. Pour mixture into a chilled soup tureen. Stir in chives, cayenne, salt and pepper. Refrigerate, covered, for several hours before serving.

Chilled Grilled Red Pepper Soup with Crème Fraîche

Serves 6

The vibrant hue and intense flavor of this soup will have everyone begging for the recipe.

To make this easy soup even easier, char-grill the peppers the day before. Simply pre-heat a lightly greased grill and plunk the whole peppers, intact, onto it. As they char, turn peppers constantly to ensure an even grilling. Remove to a baking sheet to cool for 1 to 2 minutes. Then, before they cool completely, place in a paper bag to steam for a few minutes. Afterwards, their blackened skins will slip off effortlessly. Cut open peppers and remove the seeds and stems. Keep peppers in a plastic container.

Often you will find that a reliable cheesemonger sells crème fraîche, or at least an approximation of this French concoction. If you can't find it, use this method to make a very good substitute:

Warm 1 cup (250 mL) whipping (35%) cream gently. Remove from heat and combine with 2 tbsp (25 mL) buttermilk or sour cream in a glass bowl. Mix well, cover and let stand at room temperature overnight. Give the mixture a good stir once it has thickened, then cover and refrigerate. It will thicken even more once chilled and keeps well for up to 10 days in the refrigerator.

3 cups	chopped white onions	750 mL
3 tbsp	olive oil	45 mL
2	cloves garlic, minced	2
2 cups	sliced red bell peppers, peeled, seeded and grilled	500 mL
8	fresh basil leaves	8
1/2 tsp	salt	2 mL
1/4 tsp	freshly ground black pepper	1 mL
5 cups	chicken stock	1.25 L
1/2 cup	half-and-half (10%) cream	125 mL
1 tbsp	tarragon vinegar or white wine vinegar	15 mL
1/2 cup	*crème fraîche* or plain yogurt	125 mL
1/3 cup	chopped fresh basil	75 mL

1. In a large heavy-bottomed saucepan, heat oil over medium heat. Add onions and cook, stirring occasionally, for 5 minutes or until softened.

2. Add garlic, peppers, basil, salt and pepper; cook, stirring occasionally, for 5 minutes.

3. Add stock; bring mixture to a boil. Reduce heat and simmer, partially covered, for 20 minutes. In a blender or food processor, purée mixture in batches. Pour into a large bowl. Allow to cool. Cover and refrigerate until well chilled (at least 3 hours).

4. When ready to serve, stir in half-and-half and vinegar. Adjust seasoning to taste. Ladle into soup bowls. Add a dollop of *crème fraîche* and a little chopped basil to each serving.

Grilled Corn Soup with Pesto Swirl

Serves 6

Use your grill to barbecue the fresh ears of corn in this delightfully thick soup.

If you prefer a thinner soup, increase the amount of chicken stock accordingly.

Crème fraîche is often available at a good cheesemonger or in some specialty food shops and supermarkets. If you can't easily find it, make your own by following the simple recipe on page 53.

Parmigiano-Reggiano cheese may be substituted for the Pecorino Romano if you wish.

Leftover pesto can be used as a base spread for grilled pizza, in pasta salads or spread over thickly sliced, grilled tomatoes. To freeze pesto, omit *crème fraîche* and place in individual ice cube compartments. When frozen, pop them out and store in sealed plastic bags. Use them to enliven soups, stews or casseroles.

Preheat grill or barbecue to medium-high

8	ears fresh corn, husked	8
2 tbsp	butter	25 mL
1 1/2 cups	finely chopped onions	375 mL
2	cloves garlic, minced	2
3 cups	chicken stock	750 mL
1 cup	whipping (35%) cream	250 mL
	Salt and freshly ground black pepper, to taste	

PESTO

1	large clove garlic	1
2 cups	lightly packed fresh basil leaves	500 mL
1 1/2 tbsp	pine nuts	20 mL
1/2 cup	extra virgin olive oil	125 mL
1/2 cup	grated Pecorino Romano cheese	125 mL
1 cup	*crème fraîche*	250 mL
	Fresh basil leaves	

1. Grill corn for about 10 to 12 minutes or until tender, using tongs to turn ears from time to time. Remove from grill; allow to cool slightly. Using a sharp knife, cut kernels from cobs. Collect kernels in a bowl; set aside.

2. In a large pot, heat butter over medium-high heat. Add onion and garlic; cook, stirring often, for 3 to 4 minutes or until slightly softened. Add corn (reserving 1/3 cup [75 mL] for garnish). Cook for 3 minutes, stirring frequently.

3. Add chicken stock; bring to a gentle boil. Reduce heat to medium; simmer, partially covered, for about 5 minutes. In a blender or food processor, purée soup (in batches if necessary); return to saucepan. Over medium heat, add cream. Season to taste with salt and pepper. Simmer to heat through.

4. Meanwhile, prepare pesto. In a blender or food processor, process garlic until minced. Add basil, pine nuts and olive oil. Blend ingredients together until finely puréed. Using a rubber spatula, scrape mixture into a small mixing bowl. Fold in grated cheese until well blended. Carefully stir in *crème fraîche*. Season to taste with salt and pepper. Cover and refrigerate until ready to use.

5. When ready to serve, ladle soup into bowls. Place a dollop of pesto in center; draw tip of a knife through to swirl. Garnish with basil leaves and a few corn kernels. Serve immediately.

Cream of Watercress Soup with Nasturtiums

Serves 6

This is an elegant, pale-hued soup that is delicious either warm or chilled. The vibrant colors of fresh nasturtiums play off beautifully against the soft, muted tone of the soup and their lively pepperiness helps to enhance the other flavors. Be sure to use pesticide-free nasturtiums for the garnish.

This soup can be prepared 1 day ahead up to the point cream is added.

6 cups	chicken stock	1.5 L
1/2 cup	butter	125 mL
4 cups	chopped white onions	1 L
1	small leek, rinsed, trimmed and chopped	1
1/4 cup	all-purpose flour	50 mL
2 cups	chopped watercress, tough stems discarded	500 mL
1 cup	leaf spinach	250 mL
1 cup	assorted fresh herbs (parsley, dill, tarragon, chives, basil)	250 mL
1/2 cup	whipping (35%) cream	125 mL
	Salt and white pepper, to taste	
	Fresh nasturtium flowers for garnish	

1. In a saucepan over high heat, bring stock to a boil. Reduce heat, cover and simmer gently.

2. In a large pot, warm butter over medium heat. Add onions and cook 5 minutes or until softened. Add leek; cook for about 8 minutes. With a wooden spatula, blend in flour. Cook, stirring, for 3 minutes.

3. Add 1 cup (250 mL) hot stock to onion mixture, using a whisk to prevent lumps. Gradually stir in remaining stock; bring to a boil. Reduce heat; simmer, partially covered, for 15 minutes.

4. Add watercress, spinach and fresh herbs. Increase heat slightly; return to a boil. Reduce heat; simmer for 5 minutes.

5. In a food processor or blender, purée soup (in batches if necessary) until smooth. Pour soup into pot; gently heat soup over medium heat. Stir in cream. Season to taste with salt and pepper.

6. Ladle into soup bowls; garnish with nasturtiums. Serve immediately.

Cool Tomato Soup with Basil and Mint Toasts

Serves 4

The finest, freshest-tasting tomato soup ever, this vibrantly colored dish can also be served hot.

Preheat oven to 375° F (190° C)
Baking sheet

3 lbs	tomatoes, seeded and cut into chunks	1.5 kg
1 tbsp	cornstarch	15 mL
1 cup	chicken stock	250 mL
1 tbsp	fresh lemon juice	15 mL
1/2 tsp	sugar	2 mL
	Salt and freshly ground black pepper, to taste	
1	large clove garlic, sliced	1
1/4 cup	olive oil	50 mL
12	French baguette slices	12
1/4 cup	chopped fresh basil	50 mL
1/4 cup	chopped fresh mint	50 mL
1/2 cup	plain yogurt, thinned with a little milk and poured into a plastic squeeze bottle	125 mL
	Fresh whole basil and mint leaves for garnish	

1. In a food processor or food mill, purée tomatoes. Press mixture through a fine sieve into a heavy non-reactive saucepan, pressing hard to get as much of the solids as possible.

2. Using a small whisk, blend cornstarch and chicken stock together. Stir into tomato mixture. Bring to a boil over medium-high heat, stirring frequently. Remove from heat. Add lemon juice, sugar, salt and pepper. Transfer soup to a container and refrigerate, covered, for at least 4 hours.

3. When ready to serve, make toasts. In a small saucepan over low heat, warm garlic in olive oil for about 7 minutes (be careful not to brown). Remove from heat; discard garlic. Dip or brush each slice of bread on both sides with oil. Place on baking sheet. Bake in preheated oven for 5 minutes. Turn over. Sprinkle basil and mint evenly over slices. Bake for 5 minutes or until golden.

4. To serve: Set 2 toasts (one tilted against the other) to
    float in center of each serving of soup. Drizzle with
    thinned yogurt. Garnish with fresh whole basil and
    mint leaves.

Tortilla and Lime Soup Zocalo

Serves 6

This recipe is from my good friend Chef Christopher McDonald. His love of things Mexican led him to open Zocalo, a small, totally authentic Mexican restaurant that used to sit directly beneath his stylish dining room Avalon in Toronto. Alas, Zocalo is no more, but I will never forget the wonderful lunches I enjoyed there — almost all of which began with this simple, flavor-filled soup.

Mexican oregano is totally unlike conventional oregano. It is much stronger in flavor. Look for it in South American and Latin markets. Be sure to toast the oregano lightly in a skillet over medium-low heat for about 1 minute beforehand; the heat encourages the herb to become much more developed in flavor and fragrance.

Add chopped avocados if you wish and, if your grill is preheating for the main course, grill the chicken breast.

5 cups	chicken stock	1.25 L
1	boneless skinless chicken breast	1
1 1/2 cups	coarsely chopped charred plum tomatoes, peeled and cored	375 mL
6	cloves garlic, roasted, peeled and finely chopped	6
2	jalapeño peppers, charred, peeled, seeded and finely chopped	2
1	white onion, grilled and rings separated	1
3 tbsp	fresh lime juice	45 mL
1 tbsp	dried Mexican oregano, toasted and ground	15 mL
2	small corn tortillas, cut into strips, fried until golden	2
1/2 cup	chopped coriander leaves	125 mL

1. In a large saucepan, bring stock to a boil over medium-high heat. Submerge chicken breast in stock; reduce heat, cover and gently poach chicken for 10 minutes or until juices run clear when pierced with a knife. (Alternatively, you may grill the chicken.) Remove chicken from stock; cool slightly. Keep stock at a gentle simmer. Slice chicken into very thin strips; set aside.

2. Divide sliced chicken, tomatoes, garlic, jalapeños, onion, lime juice, oregano and tortillas between 6 bowls. Pour hot broth into each bowl; sprinkle liberally with chopped coriander. Serve immediately.

Grilled Pizza with Pancetta, Porcini and Fontina

Serves 4 to 6

In rural Italy, just about everyone has a little exterior wood-fired oven that is used extensively throughout the long, hot summer months for baking pizzas and roasting meats and vegetables. Use your covered grill or barbecue to simulate these traditional ovens and make the best pizza ever!

Make sure your grill racks are clean and that you follow the method (described in step 2) for preheating the grill or barbecue.

Rolling the dough into an irregular, oval shape makes sense if you have a rectangular-shaped grill. Roll it to a rounder shape if you have a kettle-shaped barbecue with a round grill.

Many bakeries and supermarkets offer prepared pizza or bread dough. I often buy a couple of balls from a local pizza parlor. However, if you have a good dough recipe — and the time to prepare it — by all means use it here.

Preheat grill or barbecue

1 oz	dried porcini mushrooms	25 g
2 oz	pancetta (unsmoked Italian bacon), thinly sliced	50 g
1 lb	pizza dough, rolled out	500 g
3 tbsp	extra virgin olive oil	45 mL
1 1/2 cups	shredded Italian Fontina cheese	375 mL
1/4 cup	chopped flat-leaf parsley	50 mL

1. In a small bowl, pour 1/2 cup (125 mL) boiling water over dried mushrooms. Soak for about 20 minutes. Drain; squeeze mushrooms dry, reserving liquid. In a large skillet over medium heat, cook pancetta for 1 minute per side.

2. If using a gas grill, ensure that one burner is on medium-high, with the rest on as low as possible. With a charcoal grill, you can achieve a similar effect by getting coals very hot, then arrange in a ring around perimeter of grill.

3. Fold dough in half; place on coolest part of grill. Unfold so that dough is situated over cooler section of grill. Close lid; cook for about 3 minutes. When dough is bubbling on top and golden brown on bottom, flip using two metal spatulas. Brush grilled top of dough with half the olive oil.

4. Evenly distribute mushrooms, pancetta, cheese and parsley over surface of dough. Drizzle remaining olive oil and 1/4 cup (50 mL) mushroom soaking liquid over surface. Close lid; cook for 1 to 2 minutes or until cheese is melted and bottom is golden brown.

5. Using two spatulas, remove pizza from grill to a cutting board. Let sit for 1 minute, then slice. Serve immediately.

Asian-Flavored Tuna with Cucumber

Serves 4

This is a very impressive, yet effortless little preparation that will please sushi lovers. The tuna should have a hot exterior and a cool interior.

Make absolutely sure not to leave fresh tuna in this marinade for any longer than 10 minutes, otherwise the tuna will begin to "cook" in it, becoming soft and mushy after grilling.

If you will be offering this dish as a precursor to a grilled entrée, be sure to clean the grill to remove any traces of the tuna before proceeding. Alternatively, you can sear the tuna in a cast iron pan sprayed with non-stick spray and set over the grill to get quite hot. If you opt for this method, there is no need to skewer the tuna chunks. Also, reduce the cooking time by a few seconds on either side.

Salmon can be substituted for the tuna.

Preheat grill to medium-high heat

3 tbsp	soya sauce	45 mL
2 tbsp	fresh lime juice	25 mL
1 tbsp	light brown sugar	15 mL
1 1/2 tbsp	sesame oil	20 mL
1/4 cup	soya sauce	50 mL
2 tbsp	dry white wine	25 mL
14 oz	fresh skinless tuna, cut into chunks	425 g
4 cups	lightly packed *frisée* or arugula, washed and dried	1 L
1	English cucumber, cut into 2-inch (5 cm) strips	1
2 cups	halved cherry tomatoes	500 mL

1. In a small mixing bowl, whisk together soya sauce, lime juice, brown sugar and sesame oil. Set aside.

2. In a bowl combine soya sauce and white wine. Marinate tuna chunks in mixture for no more than 10 minutes.

3. While tuna is marinating, arrange greens, cucumber strips and tomatoes on salad plates.

4. Thread tuna onto skewers; grill for 10 to 15 seconds per side. Carefully push tuna off skewers; arrange over salad. Drizzle dressing over each serving. Serve immediately.

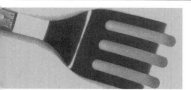

Spanish Shrimp

Serves 4 to 6

This is a classic seafood tapas dish, served throughout Spain. It can be easily cooked in a skillet placed on a preheated barbecue or grill. If you have a shallow, flameproof earthenware casserole, use it so that you can bring it straight to the table. Serve with lots of crusty bread to mop up all the lovely flavors.

1 lb	medium or large shrimp, shelled and deveined	500 g
1/2 tsp	salt	2 mL
1/4 cup	extra virgin olive oil	50 mL
3	cloves garlic, thinly sliced	3
1	small bay leaf	1
1 tsp	finely chopped seeded dried chilies	5 mL
1 tbsp	chopped fresh parsley	15 mL

1. Place shrimp in a medium bowl. Sprinkle with salt; allow to sit at room temperature for 15 minutes.

2. In a non-reactive skillet or shallow earthenware casserole, over medium heat, combine oil, garlic, bay leaf and chilies. Cook for 1 to 2 minutes; do not allow garlic to brown.

3. Increase heat to medium-high. Add shrimp and cook, stirring, for 2 minutes or until color deepens and shrimp start to curl. Remove bay leaf. Add chopped parsley. Serve immediately.

Grilled Polenta

Serves 4 to 6

There is no end to the number of toppings you can use with grilled polenta — chopped tomato, garlic and basil, grated cheese, grilled radicchio, mushrooms, white bean spread or olivada. Or, simply enjoy them just as they are with a simple green salad for a summery first course. Vary the herbs according to availability and personal taste.

You can easily make the polenta (steps 1 and 2) a day ahead. Cover with plastic wrap and refrigerate. Bring to room temperature before grilling.

Preheat well-oiled barbecue or grill to low
Baking tray with sides

3 cups	milk (or half water, half milk)	750 mL
1/2 tsp	coarse salt	2 mL
3 tbsp	butter	45 mL
1 cup	cornmeal	250 mL
1 tbsp	chopped fresh sage leaves	15 mL
1 tbsp	chopped parsley	15 mL
1 cup	grated Parmigiano-Reggiano	250 mL
	Salt and freshly ground black pepper, to taste	
2 tbsp	olive oil	25 mL

1. In a large heavy-bottomed saucepan over medium-high heat, bring milk to a gentle boil. Add salt and 1 tbsp (15 mL) butter. Stir to combine well. Reduce heat to medium-low; add cornmeal in a slow, thin stream, whisking continuously to prevent lumps.

2. Using a flat wooden spoon, stir (in the same direction) every 1 minute or so for 10 to 20 minutes or until mixture is soft and starts to pull away from sides of pan. Remove from heat. Stir in sage, parsley, cheese and remaining butter.

3. Season to taste with salt and pepper. Transfer polenta to baking tray. Using a metal spatula, spread to an even thickness of 1 inch (2.5 cm). Cover with a clean tea towel; let rest for 30 minutes.

4. With cookie cutters or the rim of a glass, cut polenta into equal-sized shapes. Brush both sides with olive oil. Place polenta on grill; cook, carefully turning once, for about 4 minutes per side or until browned and crisp on both sides. Serve warm.

THE GREAT CANADIAN BANQUET BURGER (PAGE 92) ➤
OVERLEAF: AN ASSORTMENT OF MARINADES, RUBS, PASTES, MOPPIN' SAUCES, GLAZES AND BUTTERS (PAGES 15 TO 50)

Grilled Lamb on Lavosh

Serves 4 to 6

For a truly Middle Eastern-inspired first course, serve this outstanding hors d'oeuvre with a spoonful of *baba ghanoush* (eggplant purée). Top with pomegranate seeds, a dollop of cool yogurt and fresh mint.

Lavosh is a cracker-thin Middle Eastern flatbread. In its place you can use thin slices of toast, grilled pita or crackers.

Preheat barbecue or grill to high
Shallow glass baking dish

1 tbsp	chopped fresh thyme	15 mL
2 tbsp	chopped fresh mint	25 mL
2	cloves garlic, minced	2
2 tbsp	lemon juice	25 mL
1 tbsp	hot sauce	15 mL
2 tsp	freshly ground black pepper	10 mL
1 lb	lamb tenderloins or fillets or boneless lamb chops	500 g
1/4 tsp	salt	1 mL
24	broken pieces of Armenian lavosh *or* toasted flour tortillas, broken	24
1/2 cup	plain yogurt	125 mL

1. In a small bowl, combine thyme, mint, garlic, lemon juice, hot sauce and black pepper. Mix together well.

2. Place lamb in baking dish; cover with marinade. Let sit for about 20 minutes.

3. Grill lamb over high heat for 1 to 2 minutes per side or according to taste. Season with salt. Remove from grill; rest for 1 minute before slicing thinly. Serve on broken pieces of lavosh with yogurt.

‹ CAPE TOWN SOSATIES (PAGE 130)

Singapore Satay

Serves 6

In Singapore, satays are an all-time favorite snack, whether sold at outdoor food centers, side-street grills or high above the city in a posh hotel's cocktail lounge. You can use chicken, beef, lamb or pork in this recipe — just make sure you choose tender cuts. In this recipe, the meat is cut into thin strips and threaded onto skewers. However, you could also cut the meat into small chunks if you prefer.

Be sure to soak wooden skewers for at least 2 hours before using to keep them from burning before the meat is cooked.

The peanut sauce that follows is a Malaysian-style sauce that works well with any meat. Make the peanut sauce the day before to allow flavors to develop. It will keep for some time, covered, in the refrigerator.

Canned coconut milk is available in the international section of many supermarkets, specialty food shops or Asian markets. Be sure to shake the can well before opening and stir well.

1 1/2 lbs	boneless chicken, beef, pork or lamb	750 g
3	strips lemon zest, minced	3
3	shallots, minced	3
1	large clove garlic, minced	1
2 tsp	minced ginger root	10 mL
2 tsp	ground coriander	10 mL
2 tsp	ground cumin	10 mL
1 tsp	ground turmeric	5 mL
2 tsp	light brown sugar	10 mL
1 1/2 tsp	salt	7 mL
2 tbsp	light soya sauce	25 mL
2 tbsp	peanut oil *or* vegetable oil	25 mL

PEANUT SAUCE

2 tbsp	peanut oil	25 mL
1	onion, finely chopped	1
2	cloves garlic, minced	2
1/2 tsp	crushed red pepper flakes	2 mL
1/4 cup	fresh lime juice	50 mL
1/4 cup	light soya sauce	50 mL
2/3 cup	unsweetened crunchy peanut butter	150 mL
1/3 cup	coconut milk	75 mL
1/4 cup	chopped fresh coriander	50 mL

1. Thinly slice meat into ribbon-like strips. Place in a bowl.

2. In a food processor or blender, combine lemon zest, shallots, garlic, ginger, coriander, cumin, turmeric, brown sugar, salt, soya sauce and peanut oil; process to a paste.

3. Add mixture to meat; toss to combine well. Cover with plastic wrap; let marinate for 2 hours or overnight, turning once or twice. Allow meat to return to room temperature before grilling.

4. Preheat grill or barbecue to high heat. In a small heavy-bottomed saucepan, warm oil over medium heat. Add onion, garlic and pepper flakes; cook for 8 minutes or until onion and garlic are soft and golden. Add lime juice, soya sauce, peanut butter and coconut milk. Stir to blend well; cook until heated through. Remove from heat; stir in coriander.

5. Thread pieces of meat onto skewers (leave half of the skewer free). Grill satays for 2 minutes per side or until cooked through (bear in mind that satays are traditionally well-cooked). Serve with peanut sauce.

Julia's Potato and Jalapeño Quesadillas

Serves 6 to 8

My good friend and fellow food writer, Julia Aitken, first served me these delicious quesadillas one summer afternoon hot off her back-yard grill. Think of them as a Mexican-influenced mashed potato sandwich. Just the thing for potato and chili heads — like me!

I have made these with canned chipotles in adobo sauce (in place of the jalapeños) with great results. Add more chilies if you are a fellow heat seeker.

Preheat barbecue to low heat

2	medium unpeeled potatoes, cut into chunks	2
1/4 cup	sour cream	50 mL
1 tbsp	chopped jalapeño peppers	15 mL
1/4 tsp	salt	1 mL
1/4 tsp	freshly ground black pepper	1 mL
4	10-inch (25 cm) flour tortillas	4
4 tsp	vegetable oil	20 mL
1 cup	shredded Monterey Jack cheese	250 mL

1. In a large saucepan of boiling water, cook potatoes for 20 minutes or until tender. Drain well; return potatoes to saucepan. Place over low heat to dry out slightly, shaking pan occasionally, for about 1 minute.

2. Add sour cream and jalapeño peppers. Blend potato mixture until well combined and fairly smooth. Add salt and pepper. Let cool.

3. Brush one side of 2 tortillas with vegetable oil. Place oiled-side down on a work surface. Divide potato mixture between oiled tortillas, spreading evenly and leaving a 1/2-inch (1 cm) border around edge. Sprinkle evenly with cheese; dampen edges. Place remaining tortillas on top to form 2 tortilla sandwiches; seal edges to enclose filling. Brush tops with remaining oil.

4. Grill, turning once, for 3 to 4 minutes or until tortillas are lightly browned and cheese has melted. Cut into wedges; serve at once.

Grilled Bacon and Zucchini Wrapped Scallops

Makes 20 appetizers

Smoky bacon and sweet scallops combine with strips of zucchini to make an attractive, impressive starter.

Use the best quality bacon you can find for this recipe, preferably naturally smoked and thinly sliced.

If using wooden skewers for this dish, be sure to soak them in water for 1 hour beforehand.

Preheat lightly greased grill to medium

20	medium fresh sea scallops	20
2 tbsp	lemon-pepper seasoning	25 mL
1 tbsp	chopped fresh coriander	15 mL
1/4 cup	olive oil	50 mL
2 tsp	finely grated lemon zest	10 mL
3	medium zucchini, sliced lengthwise into equal 20 strips	3
20	slices bacon	20

1. In a bowl toss scallops with lemon-pepper seasoning, coriander, olive oil and lemon zest. Allow to marinate for at least 20 minutes or no longer than 1 hour.

2. Meanwhile, in a pot of boiling water, blanch zucchini strips for about 2 minutes. Remove from hot water; plunge into a bowl of ice cold water for 1 minute. Transfer to paper towels; set aside.

3. In a large skillet over medium heat, cook bacon for about 1 minute per side or until partially cooked. Transfer to paper towels; drain and cool slightly.

4. When bacon is cool enough to handle, lay 4 strips on a work surface. Lay a slice of zucchini onto each bacon slice. Place a scallop, round-side down, 1 inch (2.5 cm) from bottom of bacon/zucchini strip.

5. Keeping scallop centered, roll bacon/zucchini up and over scallop, wrapping it as securely as you can. Secure with a toothpick if necessary. Immediately thread 2 to 3 scallops onto each skewer.

6. Grill scallops for 3 to 5 minutes per side or until just browned.

Southeast Asian Dumplings

Serves 6 to 8

Whenever I serve these truly delectable little dumplings, they set disappearance records. They are so delicious, packed with the soft crunch of just-cooked shrimp and water chestnuts — and so pretty, with the green coriander and pink shellfish shining through the wonton's thin skin. Guests just can't resist them!

These dumplings make a wonderful beginning to an Asian-inspired entrée like THAI BARBECUED FLANK STEAK (see recipe, page 88) or ASIAN FLAVORED PORK TENDERLOIN (see recipe, page 98).

For a tantalizing combination, you can pair the shrimp with any favorite seafood in these dumplings.

Wonton (or eggroll) wrappers are widely available in supermarkets and Chinese or Asian markets.

Any leftover wonton wraps can be frozen.

Baking sheet, sprinkled with cornstarch

1 lb	shrimp, shelled and deveined	500 g
1	egg white, lightly beaten	1
6	canned water chestnuts, minced	6
2	green onions, minced	2
3 tbsp	chopped fresh coriander	45 mL
1 tbsp	cornstarch	15 mL
1 tbsp	light soya sauce	15 mL
1 tsp	sesame oil	5 mL
2 tsp	dry sherry	10 mL
1/2 tsp	Chinese chili sauce	2 mL
1/2 tsp	salt	2 mL

SAUCE

3 tbsp	light soya sauce	45 mL
1 tbsp	hoisin sauce	15 mL
2 tsp	Chinese hot sauce	10 mL
1 tbsp	granulated sugar	15 mL
2 tbsp	sesame oil	25 mL
2	cloves garlic, minced	2
1 tbsp	minced ginger root	15 mL
3 tbsp	chopped fresh coriander	45 mL
2	green onions, minced	2
1/2 tsp	salt	2 mL
42	wonton wraps	42

1. Using a sharp chef's knife, chop shrimp finely on a cutting board, blending in egg white as you chop. (Alternatively, you can use a food processor, but do not over-process; the shrimp must retain their texture.)

2. Using a dough scraper or broad edge of a knife, transfer chopped shrimp to a bowl. Add chestnuts, onions, coriander, cornstarch, soya sauce, sesame oil, sherry, hot sauce and salt; stir to combine well.

3. In a small bowl, combine soya sauce, hoisin sauce, hot sauce, sugar, sesame oil, garlic, ginger, coriander, onions and salt. Whisk once or twice to blend well. Set sauce aside.

4. Bring a large pot of water to a boil. Arrange wonton skins in a single layer on a dry work surface. Place 2 tsp (10 mL) of filling on each. Brush edges with a tiny bit of water. Fold skins over; press edges together to seal. Transfer dumplings to baking sheet, making sure they do not touch.

5. Once water has come to a boil, add a little salt. Add dumplings to boiling water in batches, if necessary, to prevent overcrowding. Stir once. Dumplings will begin to bob to surface after about 1 1/2 minutes. Cook for an additional 25 seconds; remove with a slotted spoon to a colander.

6. When all dumplings have been cooked, transfer to a serving dish. Pour sauce over hot dumplings and toss gently. Serve immediately.

Spanish Meatballs in Salsa Roja

Serves 6 to 8

In Spain, these savory pork meatballs are rolled to the size of marbles and form a tiny (but indispensable) tapas.

The traditional method of preparation is to sauté the meatballs in a skillet and build the sauce around them (which thickens with the cooking time) — the perfect occasion to put your grill's side burner to good use.

Be sure to use a quality Spanish fino sherry for this dish.

If you shape larger meatballs, this appetizer easily turns into a main course.

2 tbsp	olive oil	25 mL
2 cups	finely chopped onions	500 mL
1	can (28 oz [796 mL]) tomatoes, with juice	1
1 tsp	salt	5 mL
1 tsp	granulated sugar	5 mL
2	slices dry bread	2
1/4 cup	lemon juice	50 mL
1 lb	lean ground pork	500 g
4 oz	smoked ham, coarsely chopped	125 g
1/3 cup	chopped pitted green olives	75 mL
1	strip lemon zest finely chopped	1
1/2 tsp	salt	2 mL
2	eggs, well beaten with a pinch of salt	2
3/4 cup	flour	175 mL
1/2 cup	olive oil	125 mL
3/4 cup	fino sherry (pale dry sherry)	175 mL

1. In a large skillet, warm olive oil over medium heat. Reduce heat to medium-low. Add onions and cook, stirring occasionally, for 15 to 20 minutes or until soft and a deep golden color.

2. Using kitchen scissors, snip tomatoes into rough chunks. Add tomatoes (with juice), salt and sugar to skillet; bring to a boil, stirring. Reduce heat; simmer, stirring occasionally, for 20 minutes or until thickened and reduced.

3. Meanwhile, prepare meatballs. Place bread on a plate; cover with lemon juice. Let sit until juice is absorbed. Squeeze bread until relatively dry.

4. In a food processor, combine bread, pork, ham, olives, lemon zest and salt. Process, pulsing on and off, until well combined (be careful not to over-process). Scrape mixture into a mixing bowl. Shape meatballs the size of hazelnuts. Roll in beaten egg and then flour.

5. In a heavy nonstick skillet, warm olive oil over medium heat. Cook meatballs in batches, shaking pan back and forth, for 3 minutes or until evenly browned. If there is a large quantity of fat in the skillet, pour off and discard.

6. Add sherry to tomato sauce. Pour sauce over meatballs. Allow mixture to come to a boil. Reduce heat; cook for 5 minutes or until meatballs are cooked through and sauce is thickened. Serve immediately or at room temperature.

Yakitori

Serves 6 to 8

This simple and exceedingly popular traditional Japanese appetizer cooks quickly. If you want to turn it into a main course, add separate skewers filled with squares of red pepper, mushroom caps and lengths of green onion. Serve with steamed rice and a Japanese-inspired salad.

If using wooden skewers, be sure to soak them in water for 1 hour before using.

Preheat grill or barbecue to high
Large shallow baking dish

1/2 cup	Japanese soya sauce	125 mL
1/2 cup	*mirin* (sweet rice wine) *or* sherry	125 mL
1/2 cup	chicken stock	125 mL
1 tbsp	minced ginger root	15 mL
6	boneless skinless chicken breasts, cut into bite-sized chunks	6

1. In baking dish, combine soya sauce, *mirin*, chicken stock and ginger.

2. Thread chicken chunks onto skewers; place in marinade. Turn over once or twice to coat well. Marinate for about 30 minutes.

3. Transfer chicken to a plate. Pour marinade into a small saucepan; bring to a boil. (Use side burner if you have one.) Boil gently for 5 minutes.

4. Place chicken on grill. Cook, brushing often with marinade and turning frequently, for 6 or 7 minutes. Serve immediately or at room temperature with hot mustard.

Royal Thai Wings

Serves 4 to 6

These crispy, delectable chicken wings are an approximation of those I was served in the lounge of a beautiful hotel in Bangkok where, I think, the kitchen strived to cater to North American tastes. They were totally delicious — and so are these!

12	whole chicken wings, divided, wing tips removed, washed and patted dry	12
4	cloves garlic, minced	4
2 tbsp	minced ginger root	25 mL
2	Thai chilies, seeded and minced	2
1/3 cup	chopped fresh coriander	75 mL
1/2 cup	soya sauce	75 mL
2 tbsp	sesame oil	25 mL
1/3 cup	rice wine *or* sherry	75 mL
1/3 cup	light brown sugar	75 mL
	Vegetable oil	

1. With a sharp knife, make 2 or 3 bone-deep slashes in each wing.

2. In a shallow bowl, whisk together garlic, ginger root, chilies, coriander, soya sauce, sesame oil, rice wine and brown sugar. Whisk until sugar is dissolved.

3. Place chicken wings in marinade. Cover and refrigerate for 3 to 4 hours, turning occasionally. Return to room temperature before grilling.

4. Preheat grill or barbecue to medium-low heat. Grill chicken wings for about 15 minutes, turning frequently and basting with remaining marinade from time to time. Serve immediately.

Late Summer Vegetable and Chèvre Terrine

Serves 6

Don't be put off by the lengthy assembly required for this recipe — it's worth every minute and results in a stunning preparation. If you have the time (and lots of plum tomatoes), make a simple fresh tomato sauce to pour over each serving of terrine.

Plan to make the oven-dried tomatoes a day before you prepare the terrine.

Preheat oven to 200° F (100° C)
Baking sheet, greased
8-inch (2 L) glass or ceramic loaf pan

12	plum tomatoes	12
2 tsp	salt	10 mL
2 lbs	eggplant, sliced lengthwise into (1/8-inch [3 mm]) slices	1 kg
1/3 cup	extra virgin olive oil	75 mL
	Salt and freshly ground black pepper, to taste	
1 lb	zucchini, sliced lengthwise into (1/8-inch [3 mm]) slices	500 g
1 lb	yellow zucchini, sliced lengthwise into (1/8-inch [3 mm]) slices	500 g
2	eggs	2
1 1/2 cups	chèvre (goat cheese)	375 mL
2 tsp	chopped fresh thyme	10 mL
2 tsp	chopped fresh parsley	10 mL
2 tsp	chopped fresh summer savory or marjoram	10 mL
1/2 tsp	freshly ground black pepper	2 mL

1. Cut tomatoes in half lengthwise and remove seeds. Arrange on a baking sheet in a single layer, cut-side up. Sprinkle with 1/2 tsp (2 mL) salt. Bake for 6 hours in preheated oven or until dry but still soft. Let cool; refrigerate overnight.

2. Preheat oven to 400° F (200° C). In a large bowl, sprinkle eggplant slices with 1 tsp (5 mL) salt; let sit for about 15 minutes. Wipe eggplant clean with a paper towel, then brush lightly with a bit of olive oil. Lay slices in a single layer on prepared (or nonstick) baking sheet. Roast in preheated oven for 10 minutes or until partially cooked. Transfer to a large platter to cool. Place zucchini slices on baking sheet; roast for 10 minutes or until partially cooked. Reduce oven to 325° F (160° C).

3. In a medium bowl, beat eggs lightly. Stir in chèvre, thyme, parsley, summer savory, pepper and remaining salt until combined.

4. Line bottom and sides of loaf pan with eggplant slices, layering and overlapping slightly as you go, making sure to leave an overhang of about 3 inches (7.5 cm).

5. Follow with a layer of one-third of the zucchini and one-third of the yellow zucchini. Spread half cheese mixture over vegetables. Place 12 tomato halves over top. Repeat zucchini layers, rest of cheese mixture and remaining tomatoes. Finish with remaining zucchini and eggplant, folding in overhanging eggplant.

6. Cover with parchment paper and place in a roasting pan. Carefully fill pan halfway with hot water. Bake in preheated oven for 45 minutes.

7. Remove terrine from oven; let cool to room temperature. Wrap a small board or baking sheet with plastic and set on top of the terrine. Lay a heavy weight on top to help terrine set. Refrigerate overnight with weight in place.

8. When ready to serve, turn terrine out onto a serving platter; bring to room temperature. Using a sharp knife, cut into 3/4-inch (2 cm) slices. Garnish with fresh herb sprigs and serve.

Grilled Peppers with Cheese

Serves 4

In Mexico, these smoky little peppers are called *rajas* and, as perfect as they are for an appetizer, they also make a lovely filling for soft tacos or tortillas.

Queso fresco (also called *queso blanco*) is a mild-tasting, slightly salty fresh cheese sold in plastic tubs in Latin markets. If unavailable, use farmer's cheese or dry cottage cheese.

Plan to grill the peppers ahead of time so that they can be peeled and seeded before filling.

You need just 2 cloves roasted garlic for this recipe, but if you roast a whole head, use the rest as a delicious spread for crusty bread or toss a few softened cloves into salads or soups.

Instead of roasting, you can just pan-fry one or two cloves in olive oil over medium-high heat until browned and soft. (This way you get the additional bonus of garlic-flavored olive oil!)

If you can't find fresh Poblano or Anaheim chili peppers, you can use banana peppers or yellow bell peppers.

Preheat grill, lightly greased or barbecue to medium-high heat

1	large white onion, thickly sliced	1
1 tbsp	olive oil	15 mL
	Salt and freshly ground black pepper, to taste	
4	Poblano or Anaheim chili peppers	4
2	red bell peppers	2
2/3 cup	packed fresh coriander leaves	150 mL
1/2 cup	sour cream	125 mL
2	large roasted cloves garlic (see note, lower left)	2
1/2 cup	*queso fresco* (see note, at left)	125 mL

1. Secure slices of onion with a water-soaked toothpick; brush both sides with oil. Season to taste with salt and pepper. Grill for about 5 minutes; set aside.

2. Grill chili peppers for about 6 minutes and bell peppers for 15 to 20 minutes or until softened and lightly charred. Place all peppers in a plastic bag; seal and let cool. Wearing rubber gloves, peel and deseed all peppers. Cut into strips; set aside.

3. In a blender or food processor, combine coriander, sour cream, garlic and cheese. Blend until coriander is finely chopped. Using a rubber spatula, scrape mixture into a medium-sized saucepan set over medium heat. Add reserved onions and peppers; heat gently for a few minutes. Serve warm.

Smoked Trout Spread

Serves 6

Very old-fashioned and very good, this full-flavored spread forms the perfect beginning for a myriad of grilled main courses. Serve it with bread that has been rubbed with garlic and brushed with olive oil before grilling or as the star attraction with a colorful plate of *crudités*.

Covering each portion with a thin layer of melted butter will allow the pâté to keep for 2 to 3 days in the refrigerator.

6 ramekins

12 oz	smoked trout fillets, skin removed	375 g
1/2 cup	sour cream	125 mL
1/2 cup	farmer's cheese *or* dry cottage cheese	125 mL
2 tbsp	lemon juice	25 mL
Pinch	cayenne	Pinch
	Salt and freshly ground black pepper, to taste	

1. In a food processor, purée fish fillets. Add sour cream and cheese; blend until smooth. Add lemon juice, cayenne, salt and pepper. Process until just combined.

2. Pour into ramekins and cover with plastic wrap. Chill for up to 3 hours.

THE MAIN EVENT

BEEF
Argentinian Short Ribs of Beef with Chimichurri Sauce   82
Brazilian Churrasco   84
Filet Mignon with Duxelles   85
Korean Bulgogi   86
Thai Barbecued Flank Steak   88
Texas Barbecued Brisket   90
The Great Canadian Banquet Burger   92
Vietnamese Grilled Steak   93
Bistecca alla Florentine   94
Anticuchos   95

PORK
Canadian Back Bacon with Maple Mustard Mop   96
Chinese Baby Back Ribs   97
Asian-Flavored Pork Tenderloin   98
Beer Brats on a Bun with Grilled Onions and Sauerkraut   99
Pacific Rim Coconut Ribs   100
Southern Pulled Pork   102
Vietnamese Pork in Lettuce   104
Jamaican Jerk Pork   106

LAMB
Provençal Lamb with Lavender and Honey Glaze   108
Turkish Grilled Lamb with Peppers   110
Sikh Lamb Kebab   112
Lamburger with Mint Tzatziki   114
Grecian Skewered Lamb and Vegetables   116
Rack of Lamb with Pomegranate Molasses Glaze   118

POULTRY

New Australian Grilled Chicken   119

Malaysian Chicken Satay   120

Cuban Mojo Chicken   122

Chicken Tikka   124

Pollo alla Diavola   125

Chicken Teriyaki Kebabs   126

Quail with Asian Flavors   127

Moroccan Barbecued Chicken   128

Portuguese-Style Grilled Chicken with Piri-Piri Sauce   129

Cape Town Sosaties   130

Vietnamese Grilled Breast of Duck   131

FISH & SEAFOOD

Salmon with Brazilian Spice   132

Reader's Rainbow Trout with Oregano   133

Grilled Tuna Niçoise   134

All-American Tuna Burger   136

Sumatera-Style Grilled Fish with Greens   137

Pesce Spada alla Griglia   138

Huachinango with Tomatillo and Avocado Salsa   139

Cuban Lobster Tails with Chipotle Mojo   140

Greek-Isle Style Squid   141

Lemon Myrtle Shrimp from Oz   142

Jerk Sugarcane Shrimp   143

Sea Scallops with Coriander Lemon Aïoli   144

Argentinian Short Ribs of Beef with Chimichurri Sauce

Serves 4 to 6

Beef ribs generally have a thick layer of surface fat. However, ribs are very easy to trim, so this doesn't pose a problem. Leaving some fat behind ensures really succulent meat — it bastes the ribs as they cook. I get the best results by slow-cooking ribs in a low-heat oven before grilling. It's time consuming, but the results are well worth it.

I've included a spice rub to be applied to the ribs before oven-cooking, but a simple rub of salt and coarsely ground black pepper works well too.

Chimichurri sauce is Argentina's answer to ketchup or salsa and is used for everything from dipping bread to enhancing grilled beef ribs, steaks and other meats. It is simply wonderful with grilled shrimp or fish. Increase the chili according to your personal heat tolerance.

Preheat oven to 275° F (140° C)
Roasting pan

CHIMICHURRI SAUCE

6	cloves garlic	6
1	white onion, finely chopped	1
2	bunches Italian parsley, stems trimmed	2
	Juice of 2 large lemons	
1/2 tsp	chili flakes	2 mL
1/4 tsp	cayenne	1 mL
1/2 cup	olive oil	125 mL
1/2 tsp	salt	2 mL
1/4 tsp	freshly ground black pepper	1 mL

RUB

1/2 cup	coarsely ground black pepper	125 mL
1/4 cup	light brown sugar	50 mL
1/4 cup	paprika	50 mL
2 tbsp	coarse salt	25 mL
6 lbs	beef ribs, trimmed	2.5 kg
2	bottles beer	2

1. In a food processor, blend garlic and onion. With motor running, add parsley, lemon juice, chili flakes and cayenne. As mixture starts to become chunky, add oil in a steady stream. Continue to process until relatively smooth and thick. Using a rubber spatula, scrape mixture into a bowl. Add salt and pepper. Set aside.

2. In a small bowl, combine pepper, brown sugar, paprika and salt; mix together thoroughly.

3. Rub beef ribs with spice rub. Place in roasting pan. Pour beer around beef; cover pan with foil. Bake in preheated oven for 3 hours. Cut into individual rib portions.

4. Preheat barbecue or grill to medium-high. Grill ribs for 5 minutes or until crusty and tender. Serve with chimichurri sauce.

Brazilian Churrasco

Serves 4 to 6

Churrasco is the Brazilian word for barbecue and while undeniably popular throughout Brazil, it has its roots in Rio Grande do Sul, in the southern section of the country. This is where the *gauchos* or cowboys routinely prepare evening meals set over an open fire. Today, *churrascaria* is the name for restaurants that specialize in grilled meats. In New York City, Churrascaria Plataforma has become one of the city's hottest restaurants. Here, waiters wander throughout the huge dining room, brandishing skewers and platters of spit-roasted beef, lamb, chicken and pork in every conceivable cut and joint. Each table is outfitted with a little signalling device which you use to notify the waiters when you've had enough.

Serve these grilled steaks with CHIMICHURRI SAUCE (see recipe, page 82).

If you have access to a South American food shop, look for the hot *pimenta malagueta* (malagueta pepper). Otherwise, substitute Scotch bonnet peppers or any other hot chili.

Preheat grill to high

6	New York striploin steaks, each 1-inch (2.5 cm) thick	6
2	malagueta peppers, seeded and thinly sliced	2
4	cloves garlic, thinly sliced	4
1/4 cup	olive oil	50 mL
	Salt and freshly ground black pepper, to taste	
	CHIMICHURRI SAUCE (see recipe, page 82)	

1. With a sharp paring knife, make 5 or 6 slits in each steak. Insert a slice of pepper and garlic in each slit. Brush steaks with olive oil. Season both sides with salt and pepper.

2. Place steaks on grill. Cook 5 minutes per side for medium doneness, or to taste. Serve with CHIMICHURRI SAUCE.

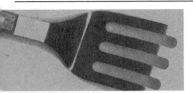

Filet Mignon with Duxelles

Serves 4 to 6

Duxelles consist of a fine mixture of mushrooms — wild, cultivated or a combination of both — lovingly minced by hand (no electric food choppers here) with similarly hand-chopped onions. These are cooked over a slow heat in a good quantity of butter until the mixture becomes thick and paste-like. In France, this woodsy mixture is used to form the basis for rich sauces and soups, to fill omelettes and crêpes and so much more. I love it tossed with hot pasta, spread onto good bread or stirred into cream sauces or soups that need a boost. It is simply wonderful when used to crown grilled fish, chicken or — perhaps best of all — filet mignon.

This recipe makes about 1 cup (250 mL) *duxelles*. Store any leftovers in a jar in the refrigerator.

If you like, you can add fresh herbs, garlic, chopped tomato or a handful of grated Parmigiano-Reggiano to the original mixture.

Preheat grill to high

3 tbsp	unsalted butter	45 mL
1	large white onion, minced	1
2 cups	minced mushrooms	500 mL
1/4 tsp	salt	1 mL
1/4 tsp	freshly ground black pepper	1 mL
1/4 tsp	granulated sugar	1 mL
1 tsp	Worcestershire sauce	5 mL
4 to 6	filet mignon steaks, each about 1 inch (2.5 cm) thick	4 to 6
	Olive oil	
	Salt and freshly ground black pepper, to taste	
	Horseradish *or* strong mustard	

1. In a large skillet, melt butter over medium-high heat. Add onion and cook for 3 minutes or until slightly transparent. Add mushrooms, salt, black pepper, sugar and Worcestershire sauce. Cook, stirring frequently, for 15 minutes or until liquid has evaporated and mixture has become paste-like. Remove pan from heat; cover with a lid to keep warm. Set aside until steaks are ready.

2. Rub steaks on both sides with a little olive oil, salt and pepper; place on grill. Cook 5 to 6 minutes per side (for medium-rare) or according to taste.

3. Remove steaks from grill. Place a dollop of warm *duxelles* on each steak. Serve immediately accompanied by horseradish or strong mustard.

Korean Bulgogi

Serves 6

Bulgogi is the Korean term for marinated, thinly sliced beef. When the same marinade is applied to short ribs of beef it is called *bulgalbi*. In contemporary Korean restaurants, specially designed conical hotplates are fitted over tabletop burners. These allow diners to cook the marinated meat very quickly on each side, which is then dipped into the intensely flavored sauce before eating.

Serve this dish with simple steamed rice and Korea's famous spicy pickled cabbage — called *kim chee* — available in Korean grocery stores. The bean paste required for the sauce can also be found in Korean food shops, stores specializing in Asian foods or the international section of some supermarkets.

MARINADE

1/2 cup	light soya sauce	125 mL
1/2 cup	dark soya sauce	125 mL
1/2 cup	water	125 mL
1	green onion, finely chopped	1
2	cloves garlic, minced	2
1 tbsp	granulated sugar	15 mL
1 tbsp	minced ginger root	15 mL
1/4 tsp	freshly ground black pepper	1 mL
2 tbsp	sesame seeds, toasted and ground	25 mL
2 1/2 lbs	beef strip loin, thinly sliced	1.13 kg

BULGOGI SAUCE

2	cloves garlic, minced	2
1	green onion, finely chopped	1
3 tbsp	dark soya sauce	45 mL
2 tbsp	water	25 mL
2 tbsp	rice wine *or* dry sherry	25 mL
1 tbsp	sesame seeds, toasted and ground	15 mL
1 tbsp	hot chili sauce	15 mL
2 tsp	sesame oil	10 mL
2 tsp	granulated sugar	10 mL
1 tsp	bean paste	5 mL

1. In a large mixing bowl, combine light soya sauce, dark soya sauce, water, green onion, garlic, sugar, ginger, pepper and sesame seeds. Blend together thoroughly.

2. Add slices of beef; mix thoroughly with marinade. Cover with plastic wrap; marinate for about 4 hours, refrigerated. Return to room temperature before grilling.

3. In a small bowl, combine garlic, green onion, dark soya sauce, water, rice wine, sesame seeds, chili sauce, sesame oil, sugar and bean paste. Blend together thoroughly. Cover; set aside until ready to serve.

4. Preheat grill to high. Place slices of beef across grill. Cook 1 to 1 1/2 minutes per side. Serve immediately with bulgogi sauce.

Thai Barbecued Flank Steak

Serves 6

Traditional flavors are given a modern twist in this very appealing recipe.

Turn this meal into an appetizer by cutting steak into thin strips and wrapping in rice paper rounds. The wraps are sold in Asian markets and packaged either in circles or stacked wedges. They are made from rice and water, are tissue-paper-thin and must be softened by dipping in hot water. Pat dry with paper towels before using.

For best results, let steak marinate overnight.

Shallow baking dish

MARINADE

3 tbsp	granulated sugar	45 mL
1/4 cup	finely chopped lemon grass	50 mL
2	cloves garlic, minced	2
2 tbsp	light soya sauce	25 mL
2 tbsp	dark soya sauce	25 mL
2 tbsp	vegetable oil	25 mL
1 tbsp	cornstarch	15 mL
2 lbs	flank steak	1 kg

SAUCE

1 cup	Asian fish sauce	250 mL
1/2 cup	rice wine vinegar	125 mL
1/2 cup	chopped fresh mint	125 mL
1/2 cup	chopped fresh coriander	125 mL
2	green onions, finely chopped	2
1 to 2 tbsp	hot chili sauce (optional)	15 to 25 mL

1. In a medium bowl, combine sugar, lemon grass, garlic, light soya sauce, dark soya sauce, oil and cornstarch. Whisk to blend well. Lay flank steak in baking dish; cover with marinade. Turn beef over once or twice. Cover with plastic wrap; refrigerate overnight or at least 8 hours.

2. In a bowl combine fish sauce, vinegar, mint, coriander and green onions. If desired, add hot chili sauce. Stir to blend well. Set aside.

3. Bring meat to room temperature before grilling. Preheat barbecue or grill to medium-high. Remove meat from marinade. Grill for 5 to 8 minutes per side for medium doneness, or according to taste.

4. Transfer grilled steaks to a wooden carving board. Allow to rest for 1 minute before slicing thinly on diagonal across grain. Serve with sauce.

Texas Barbecued Brisket

Serves 8 to 10

There are many regions in America that lay claim to the world's greatest barbecued brisket, but perhaps none with the enthusiasm that Texas reserves for this favored cut. For anyone not from this part of the world, there is a considerable amount of mystique surrounding the production of "real barbecue." Visions of digging a massive pit in one's backyard spring to mind, with masses of billowing smoke and sides of beef or whole hogs — all of which may be a bit impractical for the average urban griller. But the fact is, with a little effort and planning, you can reproduce a very reputable version of Texas-style barbecued brisket with your own grill. Soaked wood chips are the key; they are responsible for creating the smoke and additional indirect heat that encourages the meat to cook for a long time without burning.

Roasting pan

1 tbsp	freshly ground black pepper	15 mL
1 tbsp	freshly ground white pepper	15 mL
1 tsp	cayenne	5 mL
1 tsp	paprika	5 mL
1 tsp	thyme	5 mL
2 tsp	salt	10 mL
1 tbsp	sugar	15 mL
1 tbsp	dry mustard	15 mL
2 1/2 to 3 lbs	beef brisket, visible fat trimmed	1.25 to 1.5 kg
1 1/2 cups	barbecue sauce	375 mL

1. In a small bowl, combine black pepper, white pepper, cayenne, paprika, thyme, salt, sugar and dry mustard. Blend together thoroughly.

2. Place beef brisket on a large piece of extra-strong foil. Rub beef all over with dry rub. Wrap in foil, not too tightly, and refrigerate overnight or at least 4 hours.

3. When ready to cook, preheat oven to 350° F (180° C). Place foil-wrapped brisket in pan. Roast for 2 hours or until tender. Place barbecue sauce in a small saucepan and set aside.

4. Preheat lightly greased grill to medium-high. Remove meat from oven. Open foil over a bowl to catch juices. Remove as much grease from juices as possible. Add no more than 1 cup (250 mL) juices to barbecue sauce. Simmer sauce over low heat for 10 minutes.

In Texas, this cut is slow-cooked in a covered grill over a low fire for up to 10 hours! Clearly, if you choose to make brisket the traditional Texan way, this is not a cooking procedure that you can rush. Tender loving care is required for this cut to emerge melt-in-your-mouth tender.

The recipe presented here speeds things up by oven-roasting the brisket. Then it's finished off on a hot grill, attaining that classic smoki-ness Texans love.

Give the brisket a good rub-bing before it enters the oven, reserving barbecue sauce for final cooking on the grill. Use whichever bar-becue sauce you have a hankering for, (see pages 34 to 37 for suggestions) but preferably one with a tomato component — it best enhances the meat.

5. Grill meat, turning once or twice, for 10 to 15 minutes or until brisket becomes crusty and brown. Brush barbecue sauce over meat during last few minutes of grilling.

6. Remove from grill. Allow to rest before cutting across grain into thin slices.

The Great Canadian Banquet Burger

Serves 6

Bet you didn't know that the banquet burger began life in Toronto, Canada! Invented by restaurant owner Francis Deck and originally dubbed the Forest Hill burger (after an upscale area of Toronto), it was created to boost flagging sales back in the 1940s. If you want to make this a truly Canadian burger, use back bacon in place of regular bacon.

Use a cheese grater to grate the peeled onion directly over the bowl.

Preheat lightly greased grill to high

2 lbs	medium ground beef	1 kg
1 1/2 tsp	salt	7 mL
1 tsp	freshly ground black pepper	5 mL
2 tbsp	Worcestershire sauce	25 mL
1	medium onion, grated	1
6	thin slices Cheddar cheese	6
12	slices cooked bacon	12
6	hamburger buns or kaiser rolls	6
6	lettuce leaves	6
6	thick slices tomato	6
	Onion, ketchup, mustard, mayonnaise and dill pickles	

1. In a large bowl, combine beef with salt, pepper, Worcestershire sauce and onion. Mix together until well blended. Shape into 6 equal-sized patties, about 1 inch (2.5 cm) thick.

2. Place patties on grill. Cook, turning once, 5 minutes per side for medium or until exterior of burger is nicely browned. Add cheese during last minute of cooking time.

3. Split buns and toast on grill. Assemble burgers by placing 1 patty on bottom of bun followed by 2 strips bacon (or 1 piece cooked Canadian back bacon). Place a lettuce leaf and tomato slice on other side of bun. Serve with garnish at table.

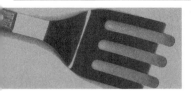

Vietnamese Grilled Steak

Serves 4 to 6

This recipe combines Asian rice noodles with Vietnamese spices, vegetables and seared sirloin.

If you can't find thin Chinese rice noodles, use vermicelli or any thin egg noodles.

Plan to make the garlic purée ahead of time. Slice about 1/4 inch (5 mm) from the bottom of a head of garlic. Brush with olive oil and place on a preheated (low to medium heat) grill for 15 to 20 minutes. Cover loosely with foil and continue to cook for another 20 to 30 minutes or until slightly caramelized. Remove from the grill and cool. Separate cloves and peel. Purée in a blender or place caramelized cloves of garlic in a small bowl and mash with a fork.

Preheat grill to hot

2	green onions, finely chopped	2
3 tbsp	rice wine vinegar	45 mL
3 tbsp	light soya sauce	45 mL
3 tbsp	garlic purée (see note, lower left)	45 mL
2 tbsp	granulated sugar	25 mL
1 tsp	hot chili sauce	5 mL
1/2 tsp	salt	2 mL
3 tbsp	Asian fish sauce	45 mL
3 tbsp	chopped mint	45 mL
2 tbsp	water	25 mL
2 lbs	sirloin steak	1 kg
	Salt and pepper to taste	
1 lb	rice noodles or vermicelli, cooked and kept warm	500 g
1 1/2 cups	blanched bean sprouts	375 mL
1	large red bell pepper, seeded and cut into thin strips	1

1. In a medium bowl, combine green onions, vinegar, soya sauce, garlic purée, sugar, chili sauce, salt, fish sauce, mint and water. Blend well.

2. Sprinkle steak with salt and pepper. When grill is quite hot, sear steaks for 4 minutes per side, or to taste. Remove from grill to a cutting board; let steaks rest for 1 or 2 minutes.

3. Transfer noodles to a large bowl. Pour all but 2 tbsp (25 mL) of dressing over noodles. Toss gently until noodles are well coated. Arrange on a large serving platter.

4. Slice steak into thin strips across grain. Arrange over noodles along with bean sprouts and red pepper strips. Drizzle with remaining dressing. Serve immediately or at room temperature.

Bistecca alla Florentine

Serves 4 to 6

In the countryside outside Florence, the white Chianina breed of cattle are legendary. This is the beef chosen for Florence's famous T-bone steak preparation. Simplicity itself — since its only partners are salt, pepper and very good olive oil — the T-bone must be of the absolute best quality, preferably prime, and as thick as 3 inches (7.5 cm). Traditionally, this steak is served rare.

Allow the steak to come to room temperature before grilling.

Preheat grill to high

1	T-bone steak (3 to 3 1/2 lbs [1.5 to 1.75 kg]) Salt and freshly ground black pepper, to taste Extra virgin olive oil	1

1. Coat entire steak with salt and pepper. Place on grill. Cook undisturbed for about 5 minutes on first side.

2. Using tongs, flip steak; cook undisturbed for another 5 minutes, then continue to cook, turning every 5 minutes, for 10 to 12 minutes or according to taste.

3. Remove steak to a cutting board. Let rest for 5 minutes before carving. Arrange on serving platter; drizzle with olive oil. Serve immediately.

Anticuchos

Serves 4 to 6

Anticuchos is the name of Peru's national dish, which used to consist of skewered barbecued llama hearts. Today, this recipe is more likely to include beef hearts or chunks of tender beef.

South American preparations often call for *annatto* seeds, a derivative of *achiote* seeds, which are fire-red in color. These seeds were originally used to adorn the bodies of Amazon tribesmen. Eventually, they were used to provide color and flavor to various foods and sauces.

Available in Latin and South American supermarkets, *annatto* seeds are used to make a spicy, colorful cooking oil to brush over the beef while grilling. To make this oil, combine 1 cup (250 mL) vegetable oil, 1/2 cup (125 mL) *annatto* seeds (or 1/4 cup [50 mL] paprika and 1 tsp [5 mL] ground turmeric), a dried chili and 1 bay leaf. After sitting for about 30 minutes, place over gentle heat and simmer for 30 minutes, stirring occasionally. Cool and strain through a cheesecloth-lined sieve. Store in a jar with a tight-fitting lid in the refrigerator.

3	cloves garlic	3
1 tbsp	ground cumin	15 mL
	Salt and freshly ground black pepper, to taste	
1 to 2	fresh chilies, seeded and chopped	1 to 2
1/2 tsp	red pepper flakes	2 mL
2/3 cup	red wine vinegar	150 mL
1/3 cup	*annatto*-flavored oil (see note, at left)	75 mL
2 lbs	sirloin, cut into 1-inch (2.5 cm) cubes	1 kg

1. With a mortar and pestle or in a food processor, combine garlic, cumin, salt, pepper, chilies and red pepper flakes until a chunky paste forms. Scrape mixture into a large bowl. Add vinegar and flavored oil, stirring to combine well.

2. Add sirloin; toss to coat well. Marinate, covered, in refrigerator overnight or at room temperature for at least 4 hours.

3. Preheat grill to high. Remove sirloin from marinade. Transfer remaining marinade to a small saucepan. Place over medium heat; boil for 3 minutes. Set aside.

4. Thread cubes of beef onto skewers (if using wooden skewers, soak in water for 1 hour before using). Place skewers of beef on grill; cook, brushing with reserved marinade, for 4 to 6 minutes or according to taste, turning once or twice. Serve immediately.

Canadian Back Bacon with Maple Mustard Mop

Serves 4

Here is an all-Canadian treat — thick slices of back bacon (also called peameal bacon), mopped with a maple and mustard sauce. Stack these slices on a crusty roll along with some grilled onions and serve with an ice-cold ale — heaven...Canadian style.

This maple and mustard sauce is also wonderful with pork tenderloin and grilled sausages.

Preheat grill to medium-high

1/2 cup	pure maple syrup	125 mL
1/4 cup	Dijon mustard	50 mL
1/4 cup	regular mustard	50 mL
1 lb	whole back bacon, cut into 4 thick slices	500 g
1/2 cup	melted unsalted butter	125 mL

1. In a small saucepan, combine maple syrup, Dijon mustard and regular mustard. Blend together over medium heat for 3 to 4 minutes.

2. Brush sliced bacon on both sides with melted butter. Place on preheated grill. Cook for 10 to 15 minutes, turning frequently. Baste with mustard sauce during last 5 minutes of cooking. Serve immediately.

CANADIAN BACK BACON WITH MAPLE MUSTARD MOP (THIS PAGE) ➤
OVERLEAF: CHINESE BABY BACK RIBS (PAGE 97)

Chinese Baby Back Ribs

Serves 4

A popular specialty of Chinese restaurants, these delicious little ribs are great on their own or as part of an Asian-inspired spread that could include SOUTHEAST ASIAN DUMPLINGS (see recipe, page 70), VIETNAMESE PORK IN LETTUCE (see recipe, page 104) and GRILLED JAPANESE EGGPLANT (see recipe, page 150).

Add some hot chili sauce or minced fresh chilies to the marinade if you like your ribs spicy.

Wrapping in foil helps ribs cook quickly and stay moist.

3/4 cup	ketchup	175 mL
1/4 cup	hoisin sauce	50 mL
2 tbsp	light brown sugar	25 mL
2 tbsp	dry sherry	25 mL
2	cloves garlic, minced	2
5 lbs	baby back ribs, divided into smaller sections	2.5 kg
	Salt and freshly ground black pepper, to taste	

1. In a large bowl, combine ketchup, hoisin sauce, brown sugar, sherry and garlic. Stir to blend thoroughly. Add ribs, turning to coat well.

2. Remove ribs from marinade. Divide ribs between 3 pieces of foil, placing the ribs in a single layer. Reserve remaining marinade. Place wrapped ribs in refrigerator. Marinate overnight.

3. Allow ribs to come to room temperature before grilling. Preheat grill to medium-high heat.

4. Place ribs (still in foil wraps) on grill. Cook, uncovered, for 45 to 55 minutes or until tender. During last 15 minutes of cooking, remove ribs from foil. Place directly on grill to brown, basting with reserved marinade. Serve immediately or at room temperature.

< RACK OF LAMB WITH POMEGRANATE MOLASSES GLAZE (PAGE 118)

Asian-Flavored Pork Tenderloin

Serves 6

With its lean quality and relatively quick cooking time, pork tenderloin is a natural for the grill. Slicing the whole tenderloin into medallions provides a nice even grilling surface and speeds things up even more.

1/4 cup	peanut oil *or* vegetable oil	50 mL
1/2 cup	freshly squeezed orange juice	125 mL
1 tbsp	grated orange zest	15 mL
2 tsp	five-spice powder	10 mL
1 tsp	salt	5 mL
1/4 tsp	freshly ground black pepper	1 mL
1 1/2 lbs	pork tenderloin, cut into 1-inch (2.5 cm) slices	750 g

1. In a large bowl, combine peanut oil, orange juice, orange zest, five-spice powder, salt and pepper. Blend together thoroughly. Add pork; toss to coat evenly on all sides. Cover with plastic wrap. Refrigerate overnight or at least 4 hours.

2. Allow pork to come to room temperature before grilling. Preheat grill to medium-high.

3. Remove pork from marinade. Pour remaining marinade into a small saucepan. Set over medium-high heat. Bring to a boil; cook for about 5 minutes.

4. Grill marinated pork slices for 8 to 10 minutes per side, brushing from time to time with reserved marinade. Transfer meat to a platter and serve immediately.

Beer Brats on a Bun with Grilled Onions and Sauerkraut

Serves 6

Hefty sausages hot off the grill are one of the best things about owning a barbecue. Treating them to a pre-grilling beer or two makes them even more succulent and flavorful.

Preheat lightly greased grill to medium-high

4 cups	brown ale (or any beer)	1 L
1/4 cup	German-style mustard	50 mL
2 tbsp	spicy ketchup	25 mL
1	white onion, roughly chopped	1
12	fresh bratwurst sausages	12
3	white onions, cut into rings	3
12	crusty buns or rolls	12
6 cups	bottled or deli sauerkraut	1.5 L

1. In a large saucepan or skillet, whisk together ale, mustard, ketchup and onion. Bring to a boil. Reduce heat and add bratwursts. Simmer, covered, for about 20 minutes.

2. Use water-soaked toothpicks to keep rings of each onion intact. Brush lightly with oil; place on grill. Cook, turning once, for 15 to 20 minutes or until softened and beginning to caramelize.

3. Remove bratwursts from marinade; discard liquid. At 5 to 7 minutes before onions are done, place bratwursts directly on grill. Cook, turning occasionally, for 5 to 7 minutes or until nicely browned and onions are soft and beginning to caramelize.

4. Transfer bratwursts and onions to a serving platter. Remove toothpicks from onions. Lay 1 grilled bratwurst on a split bun; cover with onion rings and sauerkraut.

Pacific Rim Coconut Ribs

Serves 4 to 6

Lemon grass and coconut milk give these terrific ribs contemporary appeal.

Cut the racks into individual portions and then, using a sharp knife, diamond-score them before marinating.

For information on handling lemon grass, see page 21.

When using canned coconut milk, be sure to shake the can before opening; stir milk before using.

Preheat oven to 350° F (180° C)
Large baking dish (glass, ceramic or other non-reactive material) with rack

1/2 tsp	five-spice powder	2 mL
1/2 tsp	ground ginger	2 mL
1 tsp	paprika	5 mL
1/2 tsp	lemon-pepper seasoning	2 mL
1/2 tsp	cayenne	2 mL
1/2 tsp	salt	2 mL
1 tsp	freshly ground black pepper	5 mL
2	baby back pork ribs (1 1/2 to 2 lbs [750 g to 1 kg]	2
1 1/4 cups	canned unsweetened low-fat coconut milk	300 mL
1/2 cup	unsweetened pineapple juice	125 mL
3/4 cup	chopped coriander	175 mL
1/2 cup	light brown sugar	125 mL
3	shallots, finely chopped	3
1/3 cup	light soya sauce	75 mL
	Juice of 2 lemons	
	Juice of 2 limes	
3	cloves garlic, minced	3
2 tbsp	chopped ginger root	25 mL
2	lemon grass stalks, chopped	2
1 tsp	salt	5 mL
2	lemons, thinly sliced	2

1. In a small bowl, combine five-spice powder, ginger, paprika, lemon-pepper, cayenne, salt and pepper. Rub thoroughly over ribs.

2. In a bowl combine coconut milk, pineapple juice, coriander, brown sugar, shallots, soya sauce, lemon juice, lime juice, garlic, ginger, lemon grass and salt.

3. Place ribs on rack in baking dish. Cover with coconut milk mixture and lemon slices. Cover with foil. Cook in preheated oven for 1 1/2 hours or until tender when pierced with a knife. Remove ribs and cool slightly.

4. In a food processor or blender, process remaining coconut milk mixture and 3 or 4 lemon slices until relatively smooth.

5. Preheat grill to medium-high heat. Grill ribs for 5 minutes or until brown on all sides, brushing with coconut milk mixture. Transfer to a serving platter. Use any remaining marinade to pour over ribs or serve alongside.

Southern Pulled Pork

Serves 10 to 12

Precisely how to barbecue a pork butt can be the source of serious controversy in the southern United States. While, indisputably, pork barbecue is traditionally prepared over long-smoldering coals, it can also be produced in a conventional oven, backyard smoker, gas grill or a covered charcoal grill. If you opt for the latter, using charcoal or hardwood, you must be prepared to tend the fire for a long time, supplementing the coals with lighted briquets or charcoal from another grill as needed. And, as with the preparation of TEXAS BARBECUED BRISKET (see recipe, page 90), soaked hardwood chips are a must — they generate the hot smoke needed to slowly cook the meat through, without burning.

In this version of Carolina-style pulled pork, we begin the preparation not in a smoker, but in a heavy Dutch oven. It does follow tradition in some ways, however, as it is first treated to a vinegar-based marinade in which it sits overnight.

Aromatic wood chips, soaked in water for 1 hour
Aluminum drip pan
Baking sheet

1 1/2 cups	white vinegar	375 mL
3/4 cup	cola	175 mL
1 tsp	red pepper flakes	5 mL
4	cloves garlic, minced	4
2 tbsp	salt	25 mL
2 tbsp	freshly ground black pepper	25 mL
1	3- to 4-lb (1.5 to 2 kg) pork loin, preferably butt end	1
	Salt and freshly ground black pepper to taste	
	CAROLINA BARBECUE SAUCE (see recipe, page 37)	
	Hamburger buns	

1. In a large bowl, combine vinegar, cola, red pepper flakes, garlic, salt and pepper. Add pork, turning over once or twice to coat well. Cover with plastic and refrigerate overnight, turning occasionally.

2. Transfer pork from marinade to a large Dutch oven. Cover pork in cold water; place over medium-high heat. Bring to a boil; reduce heat to low and simmer, partially covered, for 1 hour.

3. Preheat grill to medium-high. Add soaked wood chips to fire; set drip pan beneath grill. Transfer pork from Dutch oven to baking sheet; let cool slightly. Sprinkle with salt and pepper.

Tradition dictates a good rubbing with no more than salt and pepper before the meat hits the grill, but use a favorite dry rub if you prefer. In addition, make sure to set a drip pan on top of the coals beneath the meat; this will reduce flames from fat dripping onto the coals.

Use Carolina Barbecue Sauce (see recipe, page 37) to baste the meat as it cooks. Use more of the same sauce once the meat is fully cooked — its sharp, acidic edge is the perfect counterpoint to the richness of the pork and is integral to the success of this dish.

4. Place pork on grill; mop with barbecue sauce. Close lid and grill pork, turning and mopping with more sauce, for 1 hour or until meat thermometer reads 170 to 200° F (80 to 100° C). Transfer to a cutting board; allow to rest for 25 minutes.

5. Using two forks or your fingers, pull meat into shreds, discarding any excess fat as you work. Once all meat has been pulled or shredded into large long pieces, roughly chop meat with a sharp knife.

6. Transfer meat to a large bowl. Combine with enough barbecue sauce to lightly moisten all the meat. Serve piled onto hamburger buns.

Vietnamese Pork in Lettuce

Serves 6

In Vietnam this dish is so popular that many butcher shops sell lean pork pre-ground and seasoned especially for this recipe. All the cook has to do is mold the meat around skewers before grilling.

Serve this delicious light summer supper with icy Asian beer.

Preheat grill to medium-high

PORK

1 lb	boneless lean pork, cubed	500 g
6	water chestnuts	6
1	large clove garlic	1
1	green onion	1
2 tbsp	light soya sauce	25 mL
2 tsp	vegetable oil	10 mL
	Juice of 1 large lemon	
1 tsp	granulated sugar	5 mL
1 tsp	salt	5 mL
1 tsp	Chinese chili oil	5 mL
1/2 tsp	chopped ginger root	2 mL

DIP

1	hot chili, seeded and minced	1
1/2 cup	soya sauce	125 mL
1/3 cup	lemon juice	75 mL
4 tbsp	Asian fish sauce	50 mL
2 tbsp	water	25 mL
2	cloves garlic, minced	2
1 tsp	granulated sugar	5 mL
1	small carrot, finely shredded	1

GARNISH

12	leaves Boston or Bibb lettuce	12
1/2 cup	roughly chopped fresh coriander	125 mL
1/2 cup	roughly chopped fresh mint	125 mL
1/2 cup	chopped green onions	125 mL

1. In a food processor or blender, process pork until just before fully ground. Add water chestnuts, garlic, onion, light soya sauce, vegetable oil, lemon juice, sugar, salt, chili oil and ginger. Process until smooth.

2. Using a rubber spatula, scrape pork mixture into a medium bowl. Scoop a small ball of mixture and mold into a short sausage shape. Repeat with remaining pork mixture until you have about 12 sausages.

3. Carefully slide a skewer (if using wooden skewers soak in water for 1 hour beforehand) up center of each sausage, molding firmly as you work, so meat occupies top two-thirds of each skewer. Alternatively, arrange pork on a grill sheet.

4. Arrange skewers on grill, making sure they don't touch each other. Cook, turning occasionally with tongs, for 10 to 15 minutes or until all sides are browned and crusted.

5. Meanwhile, in a food processor or blender, combine chili, soya sauce, lemon juice, fish sauce, water, garlic and sugar. Using on/off motion, blend together for 1 minute. Pour sauce into a small serving bowl. Scatter shredded carrot over surface.

6. When pork is ready, remove from grill. Arrange on a serving platter. Place lettuce leaves, coriander, mint and green onion in separate serving bowls.

7. On lettuce leaf, place a bit of coriander, mint and onion. Slide pork off skewer; lay in center of leaf. Wrap up like a package; dip in sauce. If desired, serve with additional dishes of Asian fish sauce or hot chili sauce.

Jamaican Jerk Pork

Serves 6

Long before rubs and dry marinades became popular, Jamaicans were combining chilies, thyme, allspice, green onion and other spices to make their famous jerk seasoning. Once treated to these spices, meat would be grilled over an outdoor fire of allspice branches and leaves which, inevitably, added even more aromatic intensity to the flavor. The beauty of "jerk" — which is best teamed with pork, chicken, fish and shrimp — is that it can be applied as a dry rub or a versatile paste marinade. In Jamaica, I enjoyed it smeared onto hefty lobsters before grilling — unbelievably good! For an impressive entrée, try the paste smeared over a couple of racks of lamb.

Jamaicans traditionally choose chunks of bone-in meat to make jerk pork. In this recipe, I have chosen to use pork tenderloin — with very good results.

Shallow glass or ceramic baking dish

1 1/2 tsp	ground allspice	7 mL
1 1/2 tsp	salt	7 mL
1/2 tsp	freshly ground black pepper	2 mL
1/2 tsp	dried thyme	2 mL
1/4 tsp	ground cinnamon	1 mL
1/4 tsp	ground nutmeg	1 mL
1/8 tsp	ground cloves	0.5 mL
3	green onions, roughly chopped	3
3	cloves garlic	3
2	Scotch bonnet peppers, seeded	2
1	onion, roughly chopped	1
	Juice of 1 large lemon	
3 tbsp	vegetable oil	45 mL
2 tbsp	dark soya sauce	25 mL
2 tbsp	malt vinegar	25 mL
1 tsp	chopped ginger root	5 mL
2	pork tenderloins, trimmed (1 1/2 to 2 lbs [750 g to 1 kg])	2

1. In a large bowl, combine allspice, salt, black pepper, thyme, cinnamon, nutmeg and cloves. Mix thoroughly.

2. In a food processor, combine green onions, garlic, Scotch bonnet peppers, onion, lemon juice, vegetable oil, dark soya sauce, malt vinegar and ginger root. Using on/off switch, blend ingredients until relatively smooth.

3. Place pork in baking dish. Cover with jerk paste marinade, turning pork a few times to coat well. Cover with plastic wrap and refrigerate for at least 2 hours or up to 8 hours, turning tenderloins about once every hour. Remove from refrigerator 30 minutes before grilling.

This recipe may make a little more jerk paste than you need for the two pork tenderloins. Store the remainder in a small jar in the refrigerator; it will keep for some time.

Scotch bonnet (or habanero) chili peppers give jerk its distinctive heat and flavor. However, in a pinch, you can substitute any hot chili pepper.

This pork is wonderful with CREAMY SOUTHERN COLESLAW (see recipe, page 164) and JAMAICAN RICE AND PEAS (see recipe, page 157).

4. Preheat grill to medium-high. Remove pork from marinade; pour any remaining marinade into a small saucepan. Bring to a boil and set aside. Place pork on grill; cook for about 12 minutes, brushing with reserved marinade. Using tongs, turn pork and continue to cook for 12 to 15 minutes, brushing with marinade.

5. Remove meat from grill. Place on a cutting board; cover loosely with foil. Allow pork to rest. Carve into relatively thick slices and serve.

Provençal Lamb with Lavender and Honey Glaze

Serves 8 to 10

I am a proud founding member of The Some Fun Club, established in the 1980s — a group of six good friends who are dedicated to the enjoyment of great food, wine and each other's company. This recipe (which has served as the main course for more than a few of our "meetings") originated with one club member, my very good friend Zenia Curzon. Zenia made it, I made it, we all made it, set over a rack and roasted in the oven to pink perfection.

Then one winter day, another of the club's members, Leslie Fruman, eager to show us her skills with her beautiful new gas grill, decided it simply must be barbecued. As we all sat at the dining room table, enjoying copious glasses of wine and happily anticipating the feast to come, Leslie ran back and forth in her winter coat to the outdoor grill, determined not to overcook the succulent piece of meat. A few glasses of wine later, Leslie entered the dining room with said grilled leg, looking every inch the example of grilling acuity.

Continues next page...

1/2 cup	olive oil	125 mL
1/2 cup	fresh lemon juice	125 mL
1/3 cup	honey	75 mL
3 tbsp	Dijon mustard	45 mL
5	cloves garlic, roughly chopped	5
1	large onion, chopped	1
2 tbsp	*herbes de Provence*	25 mL
1 tbsp	chopped fresh rosemary	15 mL
1 tbsp	chopped dry lavender blossoms	15 mL
1/2 tsp	salt	2 mL
1/4 tsp	freshly ground black pepper	1 mL
1	leg of lamb (4 to 6 lbs [2 to 3 kg]), boned, butterflied and trimmed	1
	LAVENDER HILL BUTTER (see recipe, page 43)	

1. In a large bowl, whisk together olive oil, lemon juice, honey and mustard. Stir in garlic, onion, *herbes de Provence*, rosemary, lavender, salt and pepper. Mix to combine thoroughly.

2. Add lamb to marinade, turning to coat well. Cover with plastic wrap; marinate in refrigerator overnight, turning occasionally. Remove from refrigerator 30 minutes before grilling.

(Continued from page 108)
As she beamed at us, and
we at her, the lamb slid
silently from the serving platter onto, and indeed across,
the gleaming hardwood floor
where it came to rest at our
feet. A deadly silence fell
over the room for about two
seconds. Whereupon Leslie
speared the fallen joint,
hoisted it back onto the platter and served it forth to her
fellow club members who,
happily, had imbibed just as
much wine as the cook. We
all agreed, it never tasted
better.

3. Preheat grill to medium-high. Remove lamb from mari-
    nade. Place on grill; cook 7 to 8 minutes on first side.
    Turn; grill 7 to 8 minutes. Repeat until lamb has been
    on grill for about 30 minutes for medium-rare or until
    meat thermometer registers 140 to 150° F (60 to
    65° C). Remove from grill; let rest for 10 to 15 min-
    utes before slicing. Serve with LAVENDER HILL
    BUTTER.

Turkish Grilled Lamb with Peppers

Serves 4

In Turkey these kebabs are served with an onion-parsley condiment and grilled green peppers.

The traditional method of slitting open the cubes of lamb before skewering (butterfly fashion) makes for a quicker cooking time on the grill.

Make the spice mixture (which, by the way, makes a great spice rub on its own) ahead of time. There will be enough for two or three more meals. Pour the remaining mixture in an air-tight jar and store in a dark, dry place.

Look for the Turkish hot pepper paste in Middle Eastern grocery stores, or make your own by adding a minced fresh chili to tomato paste.

If you can't locate dried winter savory, substitute dried summer savory and add 1/2 tsp (2 mL) dried thyme.

This recipe is wonderful served over a bed of bulgur with grilled flatbread or thinly sliced red onions tossed with fresh parsley.

1 1/2 tsp	dried winter savory	7 mL
1 tbsp	mixed pickling spice	15 mL
1/2 tsp	freshly grated nutmeg	2 mL
1 tsp	freshly ground black pepper	5 mL
1/2 tsp	ground cinnamon	2 mL
1/2 tsp	dried mint	2 mL
1/2 tsp	ground cumin	2 mL
2 tbsp	tomato paste	25 mL
2 tbsp	Turkish pepper paste	25 mL
3 tbsp	olive oil	45 mL
3	cloves garlic, minced	3
1 lb	lamb loins cut into 1-inch (2.5 cm) pieces, each butterflied	500 g
4 to 6	Cubanelle peppers or sweet banana peppers, halved and seeded, with stems intact	4 to 6
	Olive oil	

1. In a spice mill or clean coffee grinder, combine winter savory, pickling spice, nutmeg, pepper, cinnamon, mint and cumin. Grind to a fine powder.

2. In a medium bowl, combine spice mixture, tomato paste, Turkish pepper paste, olive oil and garlic. Add lamb; toss to coat evenly. Cover with plastic wrap; refrigerate overnight, turning occasionally.

3. Remove lamb from refrigerator 30 minutes before grilling. Thread about 3 pieces of lamb onto each skewer (if using wooden skewers, soak for 1 hour before using).

4. Preheat grill to medium-high. Brush both sides of split peppers with olive oil. Grill peppers for 5 to 6 minutes or until softened and beginning to char. Remove from grill to a serving platter.

5. Grill lamb for 2 to 3 minutes per side, brushing with more oil. Transfer to serving platter. Serve immediately.

Sikh Lamb Kebab

Serves 4 to 6

For many years, my daughters and I have enjoyed wonderful Punjabi-style meals at a Toronto restaurant called Sher-e-Punjab. This family-run spot has been serving consistently good food to a faithful audience for many years. Among the "appetizers" listed on the menu are spicy little sausage-like kebabs dubbed "Sikh kebabs." The lamb is ground and spiced, molded around a skewer and then quickly grilled. It is served with sliced white onion, a dish of coriander and mint chutney — absolutely delicious! This recipe is a fair approximation of those stellar kebabs.

Toasting individual spices beforehand bestows upon them another dimension of flavor and aroma. Cumin seeds, for instance, have a faint caraway-like flavor. When dry-roasted, cooled and ground, their fragrance and flavor intensify, becoming quite earthy and aromatic, influencing the meats or vegetables with which they are partnered.

Baking sheet

1 tsp	cumin seeds	5 mL
1 tsp	coriander seeds	5 mL
1 1/2 lbs	boneless lamb, cut into chunks	750 g
2	cloves garlic	2
1	onion, quartered	1
1	fresh chili, seeded	1
1 cup	cashews	250 mL
1/3 cup	fresh mint leaves	75 mL
1/4 cup	dry bread crumbs	50 mL
2 to 4 tbsp	raisins	25 to 50 mL
1 tsp	lemon zest	5 mL
1	egg	1
1 tsp	salt	5 mL
1/4 tsp	freshly ground black pepper	1 mL
	Vegetable oil	

1. In a small heavy skillet set over medium heat, toast cumin and coriander seeds, stirring and shaking pan, for about 2 minutes. Using a mortar and pestle or food processor, grind seeds to a powder.

2. In a food processor, combine cumin/coriander powder, lamb, garlic, onion, chili, cashews, mint, bread crumbs, raisins, lemon zest, egg, salt and pepper. Using on/off motion, pulse until mixture comes together but is still rather coarse. Do not overprocess to a paste.

3. Working with 1 tbsp (15 mL) mixture at a time, roll into short, sausage-like shapes, gently squeezing together as you work. Thread 3 "sausages" on each skewer (if using wooden skewers, be sure to soak in water for 1 hour before using).

In India they use a popular technique called *tarka,* which involves dropping whole seeds, spices and pods into hot oil. After much sizzle and pop, the result is a wonderfully aromatic and flavorful cooking oil. The spices and technique vary from region to region in India, making this cooking application wonderfully diverse, producing endless culinary variations on a central theme.

4. Lay kebabs on baking sheet; cover with plastic wrap. Refrigerate for 2 to 3 hours. Remove from refrigerator 30 minutes before grilling.

5. Preheat grill to medium-high. Brush kebabs with vegetable oil on all sides. Grill 5 to 6 minutes per side. Serve immediately.

Lamburger with Mint Tzatziki

Serves 4 to 6

The first time I tasted Greek yogurt, I was staying in Corfu at a cliffside inn overlooking the sea. I was served a bowl of snow white goat's milk yogurt, thick enough to hold up a spoon, with a ribbon of wild thyme honey drizzled over top. It was thick, lustrous and smooth as velvet — completely addictive.

If you can't find Greek-style yogurt, it's a snap to make at home. Look for good quality, whole milk yogurt. Set a large sieve over a bowl. Line the sieve with clean rinsed cheesecloth and add the yogurt. Leave it to drain, covered and chilled, for about 8 hours. At the end of that time, you will see the whey collected in the bottom of the bowl; discard it and scrape the thick "yogurt cheese" back into the original container. You will find no end of uses for it.

Vary this recipe by forming the lamb patties into smaller, falafel-like shapes. Pack 2 or 3 mini-patties into a warm pita along with shredded lettuce, chopped tomato, onion and mint tzatziki. Do not prepare the mint tzatziki too far ahead of time or it will become watery.

Preheat grill to medium-high

MINT TZATZIKI

2 cups	plain yogurt (not low-fat)	500 mL
1 tbsp	olive oil	15 mL
2 tsp	lemon juice	10 mL
Half	English seedless cucumber, peeled, grated and squeezed dry	Half
1/4 cup	finely chopped onions	50 mL
1	large clove garlic, minced	1
1/2 cup	chopped fresh mint	125 mL
1/2 tsp	salt	2 mL
1/4 tsp	freshly ground black pepper	1 mL

BURGERS

1 1/2 lbs	ground lamb	750 g
1 tsp	ground cumin	5 mL
1	small white onion, grated	1
2 tbsp	chopped fresh parsley	25 mL
1	egg, lightly beaten	1
1/2 tsp	salt	2 mL
1/4 tsp	freshly ground black pepper	1 mL
4 to 6	warmed pita breads	4 to 6
	Garnish: shredded lettuce, thinly sliced tomato, onion, cucumber	

1. In a bowl, blend yogurt with olive oil and lemon juice. Add cucumber, onions, garlic, mint, salt and pepper. Cover and refrigerate for no more than 1 hour.

2. In a large bowl, combine lamb with cumin, onion, parsley, egg, salt and pepper. Mix gently to incorporate all ingredients, being careful not to overmix.

3. Shape lamb mixture into patties about 3/4 inch (1.5 cm) thick. Place on grill; cook, turning once, for 8 to 10 minutes or until nicely browned and a bit pink at the center.

4. Serve inside warmed pita breads with mint tzatziki, shredded lettuce, tomato, onion and cucumber.

Grecian Skewered Lamb and Vegetables

Serves 4 to 6

There is an excellent — and very sensible — reason why Greek souvlaki is a meat-only kebab. It is because meat and vegetables require different grilling times. How often have you been served a beef and vegetable kebab with either underdone meat and perfectly grilled vegetables or the reverse? In this recipe, the meat is given its own skewer, while the colorful vegetables have theirs.

Choose vegetables according to season or availability. Pieces of eggplant, yellow and green zucchini, portobello mushrooms and small onions all work very well.

Packing the lamb chunks tightly onto skewers will please meat lovers and also help to retain the juices. For meat that is well-done, leave space between the lamb pieces.

1/3 cup	olive oil	75 mL
1/3 cup	fresh lemon juice	75 mL
	Zest of 1 lemon, finely chopped	
2 tbsp	chopped fresh rosemary	25 mL
2	cloves garlic, minced	2
1/2 tsp	salt	2 mL
1/4 tsp	freshly ground black pepper	1 mL
2 lbs	boneless lamb, cut into 1-inch (2.5 cm) chunks	1 kg
12	button mushrooms, wiped clean	12
2	yellow peppers, halved, seeded and cut into squares	2
1	large red onion, cut into squares	1
6	fresh bay leaves, snipped in half	6
12	cherry tomatoes	12
	Olive oil	
	MINT TZATZIKI (see recipe, page 114)	

1. In a large bowl, combine olive oil, lemon juice, lemon zest, rosemary, garlic, salt and pepper. Whisk together well.

2. Place lamb chunks in marinade; toss to coat well. Allow to marinate, covered and refrigerated, overnight or up to 2 days, turning occasionally.

3. Remove lamb from refrigerator 30 minutes before grilling. Pat lamb dry with paper towels. Thread 4 or 5 pieces of lamb onto each skewer (if using wooden skewers, be sure to soak in water for 1 hour beforehand). Pour remaining marinade into a small saucepan; bring to a boil for 5 minutes. Set aside.

4. Preheat grill to medium-high. Beginning and ending with mushrooms, thread pieces of pepper, onion, bay leaf and tomato onto skewers, leaving a tiny space between each piece. Brush with olive oil.

5. Place lamb and vegetable skewers on grill. Brush both with marinade. Grill lamb, turning once, for 10 to 15 minutes, brushing with marinade. Grill vegetables for about 10 minutes, brushing with marinade. Serve immediately with MINT TZATZIKI.

Rack of Lamb with Pomegranate Molasses Glaze

Serves 4 to 6

Rack of lamb is simply one of the most splendid choices for grilling. It emerges sweet, succulent, tender and juicy — especially when treated to a coating of Middle Eastern pomegranate molasses.

Pomegranate molasses is a thick, exotic concoction that you will find in Middle Eastern groceries and often in the international section of large supermarkets. It is used extensively in the Middle East and is much prized for its sweet-sour flavor, natural tenderizing capabilities and wonderful "coatability". Some brands of pomegranate molasses are thicker than others. To thin, combine molasses with a little pomegranate or cranberry juice. If you cannot find pomegranate molasses, try a homemade approximation of it by combining honey, lemon and pomegranate or cranberry juice.

Lamb racks come in sizes ranging from 4 to 8 ribs. A rule of thumb is to count on 3 to 4 ribs per person. Total cooking time will range from 15 to 25 minutes, depending on size. Be sure to turn the racks every 5 minutes or so; more frequently if they are browning too quickly on one side.

This is one recipe where a reliable meat thermometer will prove very useful. Insert it into the center of the rack towards the end of the cooking time. A reading of 150 to 155° F (65 to 68° C) is just about right for a desirable medium-rare to medium.

Preheat grill to medium-high
Baking sheet

2	racks of lamb, each 2 1/2 lbs (1.25 kg)	2
1/3 cup	olive oil	75 mL
3 tbsp	PROVENÇAL RUB (see recipe, page 26) or *herbes de Provence*	45 mL
	Salt and freshly ground black pepper, to taste	
2/3 cup	pomegranate molasses (see note, at left)	150 mL

1. Place lamb on baking sheet. Rub well with olive oil and herb mixture. Season to taste with salt and pepper. Allow lamb to sit at room temperature for about 30 minutes before grilling.

2. Place lamb fat-side down on grill. Cook, turning racks every 5 to 7 minutes, for 15 to 25 minutes. During the last 4 to 6 minutes of grilling time, brush racks with pomegranate molasses, turning racks so they don't darken too much in any one spot.

3. Remove from grill; let stand for 5 minutes before dividing into individual chops. Serve immediately.

New Australian Grilled Chicken

Serves 6

Over the next few years, I think North Americans (and indeed the rest of the world) are going to become more and more interested in the Australian food scene. The best of the new Aussie cooking is stylish and chic, always innovative and yet basically quite simple. Although some indigenous Australian foods can be difficult (if not downright impossible) to acquire, you can still apply their great style to many common ingredients. And where grilling is concerned, there is more to the Aussies than "throwing another shrimp on the barbie" — as good as that is.

This recipe captures the easy-yet-edgy appeal of Aussie food — few ingredients, fast cooking and just different enough to be distinctive. Grilling the limes caramelizes them slightly, which provides eye appeal and a lovely citrus element when squeezed over the chicken.

Preheat grill to medium-high
Shallow glass or ceramic baking dish

1/4 cup	balsamic vinegar	50 mL
3	cloves garlic, crushed	3
1/4 cup	olive oil	50 mL
1/4 tsp	salt	1 mL
1/4 tsp	freshly ground black pepper	1 mL
6	boneless skinless chicken breasts	6
3	small limes, halved	3
4 to 6 cups	fresh arugula, washed and dried	1 to 1.5 L
	Extra virgin olive oil	
3 tbsp	balsamic vinegar	45 mL

1. In a small bowl, combine balsamic vinegar, garlic, olive oil, salt and pepper. Whisk to blend ingredients.

2. Lay chicken breasts on large sheet of waxed paper. Cover with another sheet of waxed paper and, using a kitchen mallet, gently pound chicken breasts until they have a uniform thickness of about 1/4 inch (5 mm). (The thinner they are, the faster they will cook.)

3. Place chicken in baking dish and cover with marinade. Turn chicken over a few times; cover with plastic wrap. Allow to sit at room temperature for about 5 minutes.

4. Remove chicken from marinade. Grill for 3 to 5 minutes per side, depending on thickness. Use tongs to turn chicken breasts. Do not overcook or breasts will be dry.

5. Place lime halves on grill, cut-side down, to cook and caramelize slightly. Arrange arugula on individual serving plates; drizzle with extra virgin olive oil. Transfer cooked chicken to cutting board; cut into thick diagonal slices. Remove limes from grill.

6. Arrange cooked chicken on greens. Drizzle with balsamic vinegar. Serve with grilled limes alongside.

Malaysian Chicken Satay

Serves 4

If you prefer, keep the chicken thighs whole and grill them without the use of skewers.

Toast the dry spices in a hot skillet, shaking the pan back and forth to keep from burning. Then grind in a coffee grinder or using a mortar and pestle.

Kecap manis is a thick, dark soya sauce available in Asian food stores, the international section of many supermarkets or specialty food shops.

Be sure to shake the can of coconut milk or cream before opening; stir well before using.

Shallow glass or ceramic baking dish

1 1/2 lbs	boneless skinless chicken thighs, cut into strips	750 g
1	large red onion, quartered	1
2	large cloves garlic	2
2	stalks lemon grass (for preparation technique, see page 21)	2
1 or 2	fresh chilies, seeded	1 or 2
2 tsp	granulated sugar	10 mL
2 tsp	*kecap manis* (thick Malaysian soya sauce)	10 mL
1 tsp	turmeric	5 mL
1 tsp	ground cumin	5 mL
1 tsp	ground fennel seeds	5 mL
1/2 cup	canned coconut milk, light or low-fat	125 mL
	Extra virgin olive oil	
2 tsp	dark brown sugar	10 mL

1. Thread chicken pieces onto skewers (if using wooden skewers be sure to soak for 1 hour beforehand), pushing chicken towards top of skewer. Use enough meat to occupy top two-thirds of skewer. Place in baking dish; set aside.

2. In a food processor or blender, combine onion, garlic and lemon grass. Process until smooth. Add chili, sugar, *kecap manis*, turmeric, cumin and fennel. Process until thick and paste-like.

3. Scrape marinade out of processor. Rub over skewered chicken, coating evenly. Cover with plastic wrap; marinate for at least 30 minutes at room temperature or up to 3 hours refrigerated. Remove from refrigerator 30 minutes before grilling.

4. Preheat grill to medium-high. In a small bowl, mix coconut milk, together with a little olive oil and sugar until well blended. Brush skewers with olive oil. Grill 6 to 7 minutes, brushing with coconut mixture. Turn and grill 5 minutes, brushing often with coconut mixture. Serve immediately.

Cuban Mojo Chicken

Serves 4 to 6

A mojo sauce always contains juice, usually citrus and often derived from the sour or bitter orange. These oranges have a thick tough-looking orange/yellow skin and a sharp, tartish juice that works effectively as a marinade base. Look for them at Hispanic markets. Alternatively, Spanish Seville oranges (the hard sour oranges that make the world's greatest marmalade) will work well in this dish. However, in a pinch, a good substitute for sour oranges is a combination of orange and lime or lemon juice, which is what I have used here.

For convenience, the dressing can be made up to 1 day ahead and stored in a jar in the refrigerator. Bring to room temperature before serving.

Shallow glass or ceramic baking dish

DRESSING

1/2 cup	extra virgin olive oil	125 mL
1 cup	fresh orange juice	250 mL
1/4 cup	fresh lemon juice	50 mL
1 tbsp	finely chopped orange zest	15 mL
1 tbsp	honey	15 mL
1 tbsp	light soya sauce	15 mL
3 tbsp	chopped fresh coriander	45 mL
1/2 tsp	salt	2 mL
1/4 tsp	freshly ground black pepper	1 mL

MARINADE

4	large cloves garlic	4
1/2 tsp	salt	2 mL
1 tsp	dried oregano	5 mL
1 tsp	ground cumin	5 mL
1/3 cup	fresh lime juice	75 mL
1/3 cup	fresh orange juice	75 mL
1/4 cup	dry sherry	50 mL
1/4 cup	extra virgin olive oil	50 mL
6	boneless skinless chicken breasts	6
12 oz	mixed baby salad greens	375 g
Half	bunch watercress, roughly chopped	Half
1	red onion, thinly sliced	1

1. In a small bowl, whisk together olive oil and orange juice. Add lemon juice, orange zest, honey, soya sauce, coriander, salt and pepper. Whisk to combine well. Set aside.

2. With a pestle and mortar or in a food processor, mash garlic, salt, oregano and cumin to a paste. Scrape mixture into a small bowl; combine with lime juice, orange juice, sherry and olive oil until well blended.

3. Place chicken breasts in baking dish. Cover with marinade; rub both sides of chicken well. Cover with plastic wrap; refrigerate for at least 1 hour or up to 3 hours.

4. Preheat grill to medium-high. Remove chicken from marinade; discard any remaining marinade. Grill chicken for 5 to 6 minutes per side or until cooked through. Transfer cooked chicken to a cutting board; allow to rest for 5 minutes. Slice chicken crosswise into thick slices.

5. In a large bowl, toss together mixed baby greens, watercress and onion. Toss together with hands. Set to one side. Drizzle most of salad dressing over greens; toss together lightly. Divide salad between serving plates. Arrange 1 sliced chicken breast on each. Drizzle with remaining salad dressing. Serve at once.

Chicken Tikka

Serves 4 to 6

The flavorful *tikka* marinade is not unlike its tandoori counterpart, except for the addition of ground almonds and the use of chicken chunks rather than chicken joints. While I have chosen to pair the marinade with boneless skinless chicken thighs, use chicken breasts if you prefer, but remember to shorten the grilling time.

In Agra, as in the rest of northern India, bread is all-important, with some type of bread eaten at virtually every meal. And at the *dhahas* (fast food stands) some of the most popular partners to Indian breads are the lamb and chicken kebabs known as *tikkas*. Originally *tikka* referred to any one of a number of Punjabi-styled kebabs to be found in this region of India. Today, outside of India, it signifies the creamy spicy sauce in which the chunks of boneless meat are marinated before being thrust into a searing hot tandoori oven or over a grill to cook in a few minutes.

Be sure to include a few Indian-style accompaniments, like a cooling *raita* (a yogurt-based condiment-cum-side-dish of grated or diced cucumber), ripe bananas or just yogurt and fresh chopped mint or coriander.

2 lbs	boneless skinless chicken thighs, each cut into 4 or 5 pieces	1 kg
1/4 cup	fresh lemon juice	50 mL
1/2 tsp	salt	2 mL
2/3 cup	plain yogurt	150 mL
1 to 2 tbsp	ground almonds	15 to 25 mL
1 tbsp	grated ginger root	15 mL
2	cloves garlic, minced	2
2 tsp	paprika	10 mL
1 1/2 tsp	garam masala	7 mL
1/2 tsp	turmeric	2 mL
1/4 tsp	freshly ground white pepper	1 mL
1/4 tsp	cayenne pepper	1 mL
	Extra virgin olive oil	

1. In a large bowl, combine chicken, lemon juice and salt. Toss to coat well. In a smaller bowl, combine yogurt, almonds, ginger, garlic, paprika, garam masala, turmeric, white pepper and cayenne. Blend together well.

2. Pour yogurt mixture over chicken; toss to coat well. Set aside for at least 30 minutes or, if time allows, cover with plastic wrap and refrigerate overnight. Remove from refrigerator 30 minutes before grilling.

3. Preheat grill to medium-high. Thread 2 or 3 pieces of marinated chicken onto each skewer (if using wooden skewers, be sure to soak in water for 1 hour beforehand).

4. Grill chicken for 6 to 7 minutes on one side. Turn, brush with olive oil, and grill 5 minutes on other side. Serve immediately.

Pollo alla Diavola

Serves 4 to 6

I think the Italians have devised the absolute best (and doubtless age-old) method for grilling chicken. They choose small young chickens (what the French call *poussin*) and split them down the back. Then they gently pound down the breast side to lie as flat as possible, the relatively uniform thickness making undercooking or overcooking much less likely to occur. Rubbed with good olive oil, coarse salt, cracked pepper, dried chilies (*alla diavola* or devilishly hot) and a squirt or two of fresh lemon, it is then left to sit for a bit while a glass or two of wine is enjoyed. Then it hits the preheated charcoal grill — sometimes with a heavy weight (like a cast-iron pan) laid on top to encourage it to cook evenly. It is lovingly basted on a regular basis with more olive oil as it turns to a wonderful deep golden brown, crispy, delicious and addictively good.

In the south of Italy, they like to treat the split-and-pounded chicken to a marinade of white wine and fresh sage before grilling.

Ovenproof baking dish (preferably terracotta)

4 lb	roasting chicken, fat trimmed, cut down back and pounded flat	2 kg
1/4 cup	extra virgin olive oil	50 mL
1/2 tsp	salt	2 mL
1/4 tsp	freshly cracked black peppercorns	1 mL
2 tsp	red pepper flakes	10 mL
1/4 cup	fresh lemon juice	50 mL
	Extra virgin olive oil	
	Lemon wedges	

1. Place chicken skin-side up in baking dish. Rub with olive oil, salt and cracked peppercorns. Sprinkle with pepper flakes.

2. Add lemon juice; cover with plastic wrap. Marinate at least 1 hour at room temperature or 2 hours refrigerated, turning once or twice. Remove from refrigerator 30 minutes before grilling.

3. Preheat grill to medium-high. Set an aluminum drip pan beneath grill. Cook chicken for about 45 minutes, turning occasionally and brushing with additional olive oil.

4. When skin is golden brown and crispy, remove from grill. Serve hot with fresh lemon wedges.

Chicken Teriyaki

Serves 4 to 6

Perhaps one of the best-loved Japanese dishes — and certainly one of the best known — teriyaki refers to the sweetish concoction in which chicken or beef is marinated before grilling or searing in a hot pan. The sugar in the marinade helps to give the meat the characteristic crispy glaze of authentic teriyaki.

Preheat grill to medium-high
Shallow glass or ceramic baking dish

1/2 cup	Japanese soya sauce	125 mL
1/2 cup	*mirin* (sweet rice wine) *or* dry sherry	125 mL
2 tbsp	granulated sugar	25 mL
1 tbsp	vegetable oil	15 mL
1 tbsp	sesame oil	15 mL
1 tbsp	minced ginger root	15 mL
2 lbs	boneless skinless chicken breasts, cut into 1-inch (2.5 cm) chunks	1 kg
12	green onions, cut into 1-inch (2.5 cm) lengths	12

1. In a large mixing bowl, combine soya sauce, *mirin*, sugar, vegetable oil, sesame oil and ginger root.

2. Thread chicken onto skewers (if using wooden skewers, be sure to soak in water for 1 hour beforehand) alternately with pieces of green onion. (Spear onions through the side, not length.)

3. Place chicken skewers in baking dish. Pour marinade over chicken; toss to coat well. Cover with plastic wrap; marinate for about 20 minutes.

4. Remove chicken from marinade. Pour remaining marinade into a small saucepan; bring to a boil over moderate heat. Boil for about 3 minutes. Remove from heat.

5. Grill chicken on one side for about 2 minutes, brushing with marinade. Turn over; grill for 2 minutes, brushing with marinade. Continue to grill, brushing with marinade and turning with tongs, for 6 to 8 minutes or until chicken is cooked through. Serve immediately.

Quail with Asian Flavors

Serves 4 to 6

Quail are a great choice for the grill — they cook quickly (particularly when they are split, as in this easy recipe) and their sweetish flesh takes very well to a number of spicy marinades or rubs. Quail come in a variety of sizes ranging from tiny to not-so-tiny. Depending on the quail available to you, you may require more than the 12 birds called for in this recipe, especially if you are planning to use this as a substantial main course.

Using kitchen shears, cut each quail down the back. Place them on a cutting board and, using the heel of your hand, flatten them. This will encourage quick, even grilling.

Vary this recipe using cornish hens or squab, similarly split down the back and treated to a dry rub.

Shallow glass or ceramic baking dish

1/4 cup	Asian fish sauce *or* Worcestershire sauce	50 mL
1/4 cup	rice wine *or* sherry	50 mL
2 tbsp	light soya sauce	25 mL
2 tbsp	vegetable oil	25 mL
1 tbsp	hoisin sauce	15 mL
2	cloves garlic, minced	2
2	shallots, minced	2
1 tsp	freshly ground black pepper	5 mL
1 tsp	granulated sugar	5 mL
1 tsp	five-spice powder	5 mL
12	quail, split down the back and flattened (see note, at left)	12

1. In a small bowl, combine fish sauce, rice wine, soya sauce, vegetable oil, hoisin sauce, garlic, shallots, black pepper, sugar and five-spice powder. Whisk to blend well.

2. Place quail in a single layer in baking dish. Pour marinade over quail, turning once or twice to coat thoroughly. Cover with plastic wrap; marinate at room temperature for 2 hours or refrigerate overnight. Allow to return to room temperature before grilling.

3. Preheat grill to medium-high heat. Remove quail from marinade; pour remaining marinade into a small saucepan. Bring to a boil for 1 to 2 minutes.

4. Place quail on grill. Cook, turning occasionally and brushing with marinade, for 7 to 12 minutes, depending on size, or until deep golden brown and crispy on all sides. Transfer to a serving platter; serve immediately

Moroccan Barbecued Chicken

Serves 4 to 6

Morocco is the home of a popular chicken dish seasoned with lemon and mint that is usually cooked in the oven. This is my grilled variation on that traditional theme.

While I trim the chicken somewhat, I leave most of the skin on for this recipe; remove it if you wish. If using chicken thighs, increase the cooking time.

1/4 cup	olive oil	50 mL
2/3 cup	fresh lemon juice	150 mL
1 tbsp	grated lemon zest	15 mL
1/4 cup	fresh mint leaves, cut into thin strips	50 mL
2	large cloves garlic, minced	2
1 tsp	hot paprika	5 mL
1/2 tsp	salt	2 mL
1/2 tsp	freshly ground black pepper	2 mL
3 lbs	boneless chicken breasts or thighs	1.5 kg
	Extra virgin olive oil	
	Fresh mint sprigs	
	Lemon wedges	

1. In a large bowl, combine olive oil, lemon juice, lemon zest, mint, garlic, paprika, salt and pepper. Mix together thoroughly.

2. Add chicken; turn pieces over a few times to coat well, also pushing marinade up under skin.

3. Cover bowl with plastic wrap; marinate for about 1 hour at room temperature or up to 3 hours refrigerated. Return to room temperature before grilling.

4. Preheat lightly oiled grill to medium-high. Grill chicken for 5 minutes on one side. Turn; grill 5 minutes, turn again. Continue to grill for a total of 14 to 17 minutes or until cooked through.

5. Transfer to a serving platter garnished with fresh mint and lemon wedges. Serve immediately.

SALMON WITH BRAZILIAN SPICE (PAGE 132) ➤
OVERLEAF: NEW AUSTRALIAN GRILLED CHICKEN (PAGE 119)

Portuguese-Style Grilled Chicken with Piri-Piri Sauce

Serves 4 to 6

The best barbecued chicken I've ever had comes from Churrasco, a small Portuguese shop in Toronto's St. Lawrence Market. Here, weekend market shoppers line up for huge grilled chicken sandwiches on crusty buns, whole barbecued chickens to take home for dinner and those lovely little Portuguese custard tarts for dessert. The shop sells count-less chickens, cooked either on a charcoal grill or a rotis-serie, with or without their fabulous piri-piri sauce. This fiery yet flavorful concoction helps to make Churrasco's grilled chicken what it is — absolutely perfect.

Piri-piri (or peri-peri or pilli-pilli) sauce has its roots in East Africa, where it is used as a marinade for meat and fish, and as an accompany-ing sauce. In Portugal, the tiny Angolan piri-piri pepper is an important part of daily cooking. If you want to make your own piri-piri sauce, look for fresh piri-piri peppers in stores specializing in African, Brazilian or Portuguese food products. If you can't find them, any fresh chili pepper may be substituted. Wearing rubber gloves, finely chop 2 piri-piri peppers and place them in a jar with a tight-fit-ting lid. Cover with 1 cup (250 mL) olive oil and store in a cool, dry place for about 1 month.

Look for bottled piri-piri sauce in many supermarkets and specialty food stores. You may also substitute your favorite hot sauce for this recipe.

Shallow glass or ceramic baking dish

1/4 cup	olive oil	50 mL
2	large cloves garlic, minced	2
1 tbsp	hot paprika or regular paprika	15 mL
1 tbsp	piri-piri sauce (or any hot sauce)	15 mL
1/3 cup	fresh lemon juice	75 mL
1/2 tsp	salt	2 mL
1/4 tsp	freshly ground black pepper	1 mL
2 1/2 lbs	chicken breasts	1.25 kg

1. In a skillet over medium heat, warm olive oil. Sauté garlic for 1 to 2 minutes or until softened. Do not brown. Remove from heat. Set aside to cool completely.

2. In a small bowl, combine paprika, piri-piri sauce, lemon juice, salt and pepper. Whisk to blend well. Pour cooled garlic over mixture. Whisk to blend thoroughly.

3. Place chicken in baking dish. Pour marinade over chicken, turning a few times to coat well. Cover with plastic wrap; refrigerate for about 4 hours, turning occasionally. Remove from refrigerator 30 minutes before grilling.

4. Preheat grill to medium-high. Transfer chicken to a platter. Pour any remaining marinade into a small saucepan; boil for 5 minutes. Grill chicken breasts, brushing with reserved marinade, for about 20 minutes, turning frequently. Serve immediately.

◄ ESCALIVADA WITH LEMON PARSLEY VINAIGRETTE (PAGE 148)

Cape Town Sosaties

Serves 4 to 6

Sosaties are a South African barbecue favorite, consisting of kebabs in a spicy marinade. Originally, lamb was the meat of choice for these savory skewers, but today beef and chicken are used as well.

Serve sosaties with a fresh-tasting tomato *sambal*: Take 1 seedless cucumber and grate it (unpeeled) over a sieve into a bowl. Press and squeeze the cucumber flesh against the sides of the sieve to remove most of the water. Discard the water and place the cucumber in the bowl. Throw in 2 finely chopped large ripe tomatoes and 1 chopped fresh red chili. Add 2 tbsp (25 mL) white wine vinegar, 1 tsp (5 mL) sugar, a handful of fresh chopped coriander and salt and pepper to taste. Stir and let sit while you make the sosaties.

Shallow glass or ceramic baking dish

6 tbsp	vegetable oil	90 mL
1	large onion, chopped	1
3	cloves garlic, minced	3
2 tsp	turmeric	10 mL
1 1/2 tbsp	garam masala	20 mL
1/4 cup	white wine vinegar	50 mL
1/4 cup	apricot jam	50 mL
6	boneless skinless chicken breasts, cut into chunks	6
6 oz	dried apricots	185 g

1. In a skillet warm 3 tbsp (45 mL) vegetable oil over medium-high heat. Add onion and garlic; sauté for 4 to 5 minutes or until softened and fragrant. Reduce heat to low. Add turmeric and garam masala; sauté for 1 minute. Remove from heat. Stir in vinegar, jam and remaining vegetable oil. Set aside.

2. Thread chicken and apricots, alternately, onto skewers (if using wooden skewers, soak in water for 1 hour beforehand). Place skewers in baking dish. Cover with spice mixture, turning to coat well. Cover with plastic wrap. Marinate in refrigerator for 2 to 4 hours.

3. Remove skewers from refrigerator 30 minutes before grilling. Transfer chicken to a platter. Pour any remaining marinade into a small saucepan; boil for 5 minutes.

4. Preheat grill to medium-high. Grill chicken for 10 to 15 minutes, turning and basting with reserved marinade. Serve immediately.

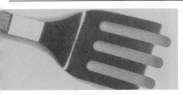

Vietnamese Grilled Breast of Duck

Serves 4

This simple, vibrant marinade is wonderful with duck, allowing the rich flavors of the meat to shine through.

Shallow glass or ceramic baking dish
Aluminum drip pan

2 tbsp	vegetable oil	25 mL
1/4 cup	white wine vinegar	50 mL
1/4 cup	chopped fresh mint	50 mL
1/4 cup	chopped fresh coriander	50 mL
2 tbsp	minced ginger root	25 mL
2 tsp	Tabasco sauce	10 mL
1 tsp	salt	5 mL
4	boneless duck breast halves, trimmed of excess fat	4

1. In a small bowl, whisk together oil and vinegar. Add mint, coriander, ginger root, Tabasco sauce and salt. Whisk to blend well.

2. Place duck breasts in baking dish. Pour marinade over duck, turning once or twice to coat well. Cover with plastic wrap. Marinate in refrigerator overnight or at least 8 hours.

3. Remove duck from refrigerator 30 minutes before grilling. Pat duck breasts dry with paper towels. Pour remaining marinade in a small saucepan; boil for 5 minutes.

4. Preheat grill to high. Set an aluminum drip pan beneath grill. Place duck breasts skin-side down on grill. Cook for 4 to 5 minutes on one side, brushing with reserved marinade. Turn; cook 4 to 5 minutes, continuing to brush with marinade. Continue to turn and cook breasts, brushing with marinade, for a total of 20 to 25 minutes or until juices run clear.

5. Remove duck from grill to a cutting board. Allow to rest for 5 minutes. Thinly slice duck on an angle. Serve immediately.

Salmon with Brazilian Spice

Serves 6

Tuna, swordfish or halibut can be substituted for the salmon, as they all have the depth of flavor required to stand up to the personality of this spicy rub. Team this with SALSA BUTTER (see recipe, on page 44.)

Be careful not to marinate longer than 30 minutes or the citrus will start to "cook" the fish.

Preheat lightly greased grill to medium-high
Shallow glass or ceramic baking dish

2	cloves garlic, minced	2
1/4 cup	fresh lemon juice	50 mL
1/2 cup	fresh orange juice	125 mL
1 tbsp	minced orange zest	15 mL
2 tbsp	light brown sugar	25 mL
1 to 2 tsp	cayenne	5 to 10 mL
4	bay leaves, ground	4
	Salt and freshly ground black pepper, to taste	
6	salmon fillets, each 1 inch (2.5 cm) thick	6
	Olive oil	
	Lemon wedges	

1. In a bowl combine garlic, lemon juice, orange juice, orange zest, brown sugar, cayenne, bay leaves, salt and pepper. Whisk together well.

2. Lay fish in baking dish. Pour marinade over fish, turning to coat well. Cover with plastic wrap; marinate for 30 minutes, turning once or twice.

3. Remove fish from baking dish, discarding any remaining marinade. Brush a little olive oil on both sides of fillets. Place fish on grill, skin-side down. Cook, turning once, for 8 to 10 minutes or according to taste. Serve immediately with fresh lemon wedges.

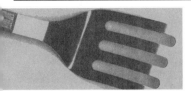

Reader's Rainbow Trout with Oregano

Serves 4 to 6

If degrees could be awarded for grilling acuity, my buddy Chef Ted Reader would have a B.B.Q. Ph.D. This king of the grill has taught me that it is possible to grill anything — from pizza to pears. Here's his wonderful recipe, which makes quite the dramatic presentation — a whole fish on a grill. It relies on the freshness of the fish and a big bunch of fresh oregano to make it a hit.

Preheat grill to medium
Shallow baking dish
Grill basket or grill sheet

2	rainbow trout, each about 2 lbs (1 kg), with 3 diagonal slashes cut on both sides	2
	Olive oil	
1 cup	chopped fresh oregano	250 mL
4	shallots, minced	4
4	cloves garlic, minced	4
1/2 cup	fresh lime juice	125 mL
	Salt and freshly ground black pepper, to taste	
	Lime wedges	

1. Lay fish in baking dish. Rub well with olive oil. In a small bowl, combine oregano, shallots and garlic. Pat mixture all over fish and well into slash cavities.

2. Leave fish to marinate for 30 minutes. Drizzle lime juice over fish. Season with salt and pepper. Transfer fish to grill basket. Cook for 5 to 7 minutes per side, no more than 15 minutes total. Serve immediately with fresh lime wedges.

Grilled Tuna Niçoise

Serves 4

A contemporary variation on the classic French salad. Here, grilled tuna steaks are combined with grilled new potatoes, fresh green beans, firm red tomatoes, capers and black olives. You need little else alongside this big main course salad other than a warm baguette, well-chilled Sauvignon Blanc and a sizzling summer afternoon.

To hasten the cooking process, parboil or microwave the potatoes before grilling.

Preheat grill to medium-high

12	baby red potatoes	12
2 tbsp	olive oil	25 mL
1/2 tsp	salt	2 mL
1/4 tsp	freshly ground black pepper	1 mL
1 1/2 lbs	thin green beans, trimmed	750 g
1/3 cup	fresh lemon juice	75 mL
1/2 cup	olive oil	125 mL
1 tbsp	Dijon mustard	15 mL
2	cloves garlic, minced	2
1/4 cup	chopped fresh chives	50 mL
1	red onion, chopped	1
1/4 cup	drained capers	50 mL
1/2 cup	whole black olives	125 mL
4	tuna steaks, each 1 inch (2.5 cm) thick	4
	Olive oil	
4	large ripe tomatoes, quartered	4
3	hard-boiled eggs, quartered	3
1/4 cup	chopped fresh parsley	50 mL

1. In a saucepan of boiling salted water, cook potatoes with skins on for 10 to 12 minutes or until tender. Drain. Toss potatoes with olive oil, salt and pepper.

2. Place potatoes in grill basket. Cook for 3 to 5 minutes, turning periodically, or until potatoes are lightly charred. Remove from direct heat.

3. In a saucepan of boiling water, cook green beans for 2 to 3 minutes or until tender-crisp. Drain; plunge beans into ice water. Drain again and set aside.

4. In a small bowl, whisk together lemon juice, olive oil, Dijon mustard, garlic and chives. In another bowl, combine potatoes, beans, onions, capers and olives. Set aside.

5. Brush tuna steaks with a little olive oil on both sides. Grill, turning once, for 10 to 12 minutes in total. Transfer to a cutting board; let rest for 1 minute.

6. Pour vinaigrette over potato mixture; toss together gently. Season to taste with salt and pepper. Arrange on a large serving platter.

7. Cut tuna into large pieces; arrange over salad. Garnish with tomatoes, eggs and parsley. Serve immediately.

All-American Tuna Burger

Serves 4

I've dubbed this innovation "All-American" because the first time I enjoyed a tuna burger was at New York's fabulous Union Square Café. Chef and owner Michael Romano buys so much fresh tuna (because of demand for his famous Grilled Marinated "Fillet Mignon" of Tuna) that he had to find a way to use up the valuable bits left over after trimming. *Voila!* — his Yellowfin Tuna Burger was born.

You will need about 1 lb (500 g) fresh tuna for this recipe. Be sure to chop the fish by hand using a sharp chef's knife. Chopping in a food processor is not recommended.

Because these burgers are relatively fragile, you may want to use a cast iron skillet to "grill" them. Place skillet on the grill and allow it to get hot before using. If, however, you feel your burgers are holding up well after the chilling time in the refrigerator, cook them directly on a well-greased, preheated grill.

Preheat grill to medium-high

1 cup	fresh bread crumbs	250 mL
1	egg	1
1 tbsp	soya sauce	15 mL
2	shallots, minced	2
1	green onion, minced	1
1 tsp	grated ginger root	5 mL
1 tsp	lime zest, minced	5 mL
2 tbsp	freshly chopped coriander	25 mL
1/4 to 1/2 tsp	cayenne	1 to 2 mL
1 lb	fresh yellowfin tuna, finely chopped (see note, at left)	500 g
1/2 tsp	salt	2 mL
1/4 tsp	freshly ground black pepper	1 mL
8	slices grilled French bread	8
	Garnish: tomato slices, arugula and mayonnaise	

1. In a large bowl, combine bread crumbs and egg. Mix together well. Add soya sauce, shallots, green onion, ginger root, lime zest, coriander and cayenne. Blend well with a fork.

2. Add chopped tuna; combine well. Shape into four 1-inch (2.5 cm) patties. Transfer patties to a plate. Cover with plastic wrap; place in freezer for 15 minutes to firm.

3. Place patties on grill. Cook for about 8 minutes in total, turning once.

4. Serve on grilled French bread slices, with tomato, arugula and a smear of mayonnaise.

Sumatera-Style Grilled Fish with Greens

Serves 4

I discovered this recipe while in Singapore. The spice paste holds influences from the Strait of Malacca, as well as Singapore and Indonesia in general.

Snapper, haddock and pickerel work best in this recipe.

For information on the handling of lemon grass, see page 21.

Preheat grill to medium-high
Grill sheet, lightly greased

1 tbsp	chopped ginger root	15 mL
1	onion, peeled and quartered	1
2	fresh hot chilies, seeded	2
1/2 tsp	salt	2 mL
1/2 tsp	granulated sugar	2 mL
1/2 tsp	turmeric	2 mL
2 cups	low-fat coconut milk	500 mL
2	stalks lemon grass, chopped	2
4	fish fillets, each 6 to 7 oz (175 to 210 g)	4
	Olive oil	
8 oz	spinach, roughly chopped	250 g

1. In a food processor or blender, combine ginger root, onion, chilies, salt, sugar, turmeric and 1/2 cup (125 mL) coconut milk. Process to a smooth paste.

2. Using a rubber spatula, transfer mixture to a skillet over medium heat. Add remaining coconut milk; blend well. Gently bring to a boil. Reduce heat; add lemon grass. Simmer for about 10 minutes, stirring frequently. Remove from heat; set aside.

3. Brush fish fillets with olive oil. Place on grill sheet. Cook for 6 to 8 minutes in total, turning once or twice.

4. Meanwhile, strain mixture in skillet through a sieve into a bowl. Return mixture to skillet. Bring back to a boil; reduce heat immediately. Add spinach; cook for 1 to 2 minutes.

5. Transfer fish to a serving platter. Cover with sauce. Serve immediately.

Pesce Spada alla Griglia

Serves 4 to 6

Every time I travel throughout Italy, I marvel at the number of outdoor brick grills, fire-places with spit-roasting features and wood-fired ovens that every home seems to have. It only makes sense, in a country that enjoys much hot weather, that home cooks choose outdoor grilling over indoor cooking whenever possible. Italian cooks grill vegetables, meats, fish, seafood, bread and just about anything you can imagine. This recipe is one of the best things about cooking — as the Italians say — *alla griglia* (on the grill.) Simple, fast, effective and delicious.

Shallow glass or ceramic baking dish

1/4 cup	olive oil	50 mL
1/4 cup	chopped fresh mint	50 mL
2	cloves garlic, minced	2
1/2 tsp	salt	2 mL
1/4 tsp	freshly ground black pepper	1 mL
2 lbs	swordfish steaks, about 1 inch (2.5 cm) thick	1 kg
	Lemon wedges	

1. In a small bowl, combine olive oil, mint, garlic, salt and pepper.

2. Place swordfish steaks in baking dish. Using a rubber spatula, scrape marinade over fish, coating well. Cover with plastic wrap; marinate in refrigerator for 3 to 4 hours. Remove fish from refrigerator 30 minutes before grilling.

3. Preheat lightly greased grill to high. Remove fish from marinade; place on grill. Reduce heat slightly. Cook fish for 10 to 12 minutes in total, turning once. Serve immediately with fresh lemon wedges.

Huachinango with Tomatillo and Avocado Salsa

Serves 4

Huachinango is the wonderful-sounding Mexican name for snapper. In Mexico this recipe is often prepared using the traditional Yucatan method of grilling the whole fish over banana leaves.

Use a grill basket or a cast iron skillet if fish fillets are particularly fragile.

Preheat grill to medium-high
Shallow glass or ceramic baking dish

4	snapper fillets (about 2 lbs [1 kg] in total)	4
1/4 cup	lime juice	50 mL
1/4 cup	tequila	50 mL
8 oz	tomatillos, husked, washed and chopped	250 g
3	cloves garlic, minced	3
2	green onions, finely chopped	2
1	white onion, finely chopped	1
2 tbsp	chopped fresh coriander	25 mL
2	large avocados, peeled, halved, pitted and cut into chunks	2
1/4 cup	fresh lime juice	50 mL
	Salt and freshly ground black pepper, to taste	
	Olive oil	
	Sour cream	
	Grilled corn tortillas	

1. Place fish in baking dish. Pour lime juice and tequila over fillets, turning to coat well. Marinate for about 30 minutes.

2. In a bowl combine tomatillos, garlic, green onions, white onion and coriander. Add avocados, lime juice, salt and pepper. Gently toss mixture together. Cover with plastic wrap; set to one side while you prepare the fish.

3. Remove fish from marinade. Pat dry with paper towels. Brush fish with olive oil on both sides. Grill, turning once, for 6 to 8 minutes, brushing with olive oil.

4. Transfer fish to a serving platter. Serve with salsa, a dollop of sour cream and grilled corn tortillas alongside.

Cuban Lobster Tails with Chipotle Mojo

Serves 4 to 6

Heavily influenced by Nuevo Latino cooking, these succulent lobster tails are quickly grilled and licked with a smoky chili and citrus mojo.

If using frozen lobster tails, thaw before grilling.

To prevent the tail from curling on the grill, bend each one backward toward the shell and give it a good crack.

Preheat grill to medium-high

1/4 cup	fresh lemon juice	50 mL
1 cup	fresh orange juice	250 mL
1 tsp	finely grated orange zest	5 mL
2 tbsp	canned chipotle chilies in adobo sauce	25 mL
1 tsp	brown sugar	5 mL
1 tsp	salt	5 mL
1/2 cup	olive oil	125 mL
6	medium-sized fresh or frozen lobster tails	6
	Orange slices	
	Watercress	

1. In a blender or food processor, combine lemon juice, orange juice, orange zest, chipotles (and their sauce), brown sugar and salt. Process until smooth. With motor running, add olive oil gradually until fully incorporated and mixture is smooth. Pour into a small bowl; set aside.

2. With a sharp chef's knife, cut lobster tails in half, lengthwise, to expose meat. Brush some mojo vinaigrette onto meat side of lobster tails. Place meat-side down on grill. Cook for about 3 minutes. Turn tails meat-side up; brush liberally with additional mojo vinaigrette. Grill for 2 to 3 minutes or until meat is opaque.

3. Transfer lobster tails to serving platter. Serve immediately or at room temperature. Garnish with orange slices and watercress.

Greek-Isle Style Squid

Serves 4

The Greeks are great grillers — their skill extending far beyond the ubiquitous souvlaki, as this simple preparation attests. If you ever find yourself on a Greek isle and are presented with the opportunity to enjoy fresh-caught calamares (or, for that matter, octopus) in a local *taverna*, order it with gusto — and a bottle of whatever the local white wine is. Just like Shirley Valentine, you may find it could change your life.

Squid takes no time at all on the grill. In fact, a professional chef once told me that the rule of thumb for squid is to grill it for 1 1/2 to 2 minutes on each side and it will be tender and perfect. If you become distracted and go past that time it will become tough and leathery. At this point, you are supposed to leave it on the grill for another 15 minutes and it will become tender again! (Note: this time generally refers to flat pieces of squid; if you purchase squid "tubes" increase the grilling time to 2 minutes per side.)

Be sure to remove the squid from the refrigerator 30 minutes before grilling.

GREEK ORZO SALAD (see recipe, page 170) makes an excellent accompaniment to this squid.

Preheat lightly greased grill to high
Shallow glass or ceramic baking dish

3/4 cup	dry white wine	175 mL
1/4 cup	olive oil	50 mL
6	fresh bay leaves, cut into strips	6
	Zest of 1 lemon, cut into thin strips	
1/4 cup	fresh lemon juice	50 mL
2	shallots, minced	2
1/2 tsp	salt	2 mL
1/4 tsp	freshly ground black pepper	1 mL
2 lbs	cleaned squid	1 kg

1. In a saucepan, combine white wine, olive oil, bay leaves, lemon zest, lemon juice, shallots, salt and pepper. Whisk to blend well. Bring mixture to a boil. Reduce heat; simmer for a few minutes. Set aside to cool.

2. Place squid in baking dish. Cover with completely cooled marinade, turning to coat well. Marinate for 30 minutes, no longer than 1 hour.

3. Using tongs, transfer squid to grill. Cook for about 2 minutes per side. Pour remaining marinade in a saucepan; boil a few minutes. Serve squid immediately with sauce alongside.

Lemon Myrtle Shrimp from Oz

Serves 4

This recipe comes from David Evans, an Australian-born chef who now makes Canada his home. Under the name Bush Dreams, he imports unique Australian spices and herbs —what he calls "Native Australian Flavours" — that lend a whole new dimension to North American cooking.

As the foods and cooking styles from Down Under grow in popularity, start look-ing for Australian spices and dried herbs in speciality food shops. Things like native pepperberry, native thyme (which boasts a tarragon, thyme and rosemary flavor combination) and lemon myrtle, come only from Australia. Intensely flavored and quite other-worldly, they can give a real boost to sim-ple grilled foods.

If you can't find lemon myr-tle, use a 1/2 tsp (2 mL) of finely chopped lemon zest combined with the same amount of dried sage and dried thyme.

Recommendations from the chef: "This marinade is good for scallops and fish, too. I suggest grilling a selection of shrimp, scallop and a small piece of swordfish per guest, and arrange on top of tossed dressed mixed greens (a dressing with an Asian accent would be perfect). If you use smaller-sized shrimp, thread them on skewers so they don't fall through the grill."

Shallow glass or ceramic baking dish

3 tbsp	vegetable oil	45 mL
1 tsp	lemon myrtle (see note, at left)	5 mL
1	clove garlic, minced	1
1 tsp	chopped ginger root	5 mL
1 tbsp	*mirin* (rice wine) *or* dry sherry	15 mL
1 tbsp	tamari (thick dark soya sauce) Salt and freshly ground black pepper to taste	15 mL
1/2 tsp	brown sugar	2 mL
12	king size tiger shrimp, peeled and split open	12

1. In a saucepan heat oil over low heat. Add lemon myrtle, garlic and ginger; heat gently for 1 minute. Remove from heat; set aside to cool.

2. Once oil is cooled to room temperature, add *mirin*, tamari, salt, pepper and brown sugar. Stir until sugar is completely dissolved.

3. Place shrimp in baking dish. Pour marinade over, turn-ing to coat well. Cover and marinate, refrigerated, for 3 hours.

4. Preheat lightly greased grill to medium-high. Remove shrimp from marinade; place on grill. Cook for 4 to 6 minutes, turning once and basting with remaining marinade. Be careful not to overcook or shrimp will toughen. Serve immediately.

Jerk Sugarcane Shrimp

Serves 4

Here is another dish that was developed by Chef Ted Reader. I decided to add the creaminess of coconut milk to the marinade to pump up the Jamaican influence.

Keep the shrimp's shell intact, but slit it down the back to allow the marinade to penetrate.

Look for fresh sugarcane at West Indian or Latin American markets or substitute regular skewers. As always, if using wooden skewers, soak in water for an hour before using.

To make sugarcane skewers: cut sugarcane in half lengthwise. Using a serrated knife, scrape away the pulpy interior. Cut the halves lengthwise into quarters to make 8 skewers.

Sugarcane skewers (see note, at left) *or* regular skewers

2/3 cup	MOBAY JERK RUB (see recipe, page 22) or JAMAICAN JERK PORK RUB (see recipe, page 106)	150 mL
1/3 cup	canned coconut milk	75 mL
1 lb	large shrimp	500 g
	Fresh lime wedges	

1. In a bowl combine marinade or rub with coconut milk, blending well. Add shrimp to marinade; toss to coat well. Allow to sit for 1 hour.

2. Thread 4 marinated shrimp closely together on each skewer (if using wooden skewers, make sure to soak in water for 30 minutes beforehand).

3. Preheat grill to medium-high. Grill shrimp for 3 minutes per side. Serve with fresh lime wedges.

Sea Scallops with Coriander Lemon Aïoli

Serves 4

To make a truly elegant presentation, thread the scallops onto dried rosemary branches instead of regular skewers. The sweet grilled scallops contrast nicely with the citrus-garlic mayonnaise which, by the way, is a snap to make — whether in a blender, food processor or by hand with a good whisk.

Make sure the eggs you use are as fresh as possible.

Make aïoli ahead of time to allow flavors to develop.

Preheat grill to medium-high

2	large egg yolks	2
1/4 cup	fresh lemon juice	50 mL
4	cloves garlic, minced	4
1/2 tsp	sea salt	2 mL
1 tbsp	freshly grated lemon zest	15 mL
1/4 tsp	white pepper	1 mL
1/2 to 3/4 cup	extra virgin olive oil	125 to 175 mL
1/2 cup	chopped fresh coriander	125 mL
2 lbs	sea scallops	1 kg
12	cherry tomatoes	12
1/4 cup	olive oil	50 mL
2 tbsp	balsamic vinegar	25 mL
2	cloves garlic, minced	2
1/4 cup	fresh lemon juice	50 mL
1/2 tsp	salt	2 mL
1/4 tsp	freshly ground black pepper	1 mL

1. In a blender combine egg yolks, lemon juice, garlic, sea salt, lemon zest and white pepper. With motor running, slowly drizzle in olive oil. Continue to blend until mixture becomes creamy.

2. With a spatula, scrape mixture into a bowl; fold in coriander. If not using immediately, cover and refrigerate. Remove aïoli from refrigerator 30 minutes before serving.

3. Thread 4 scallops and 2 tomatoes onto each skewer. Lay in baking dish.

4. In a small bowl, combine olive oil, balsamic vinegar, garlic, lemon juice, salt and pepper. Whisk to blend well. Brush mixture over skewers, turning to coat well.

5. Place skewers on grill. Brush again with marinade. Close lid; cook for 2 minutes. Lift lid, turn skewers over, brush with marinade. Close lid; cook for 2 to 3 minutes. Scallops should have a firm exterior.

6. Transfer skewers to a serving platter. Serve with Coriander Lemon Aïoli alongside.

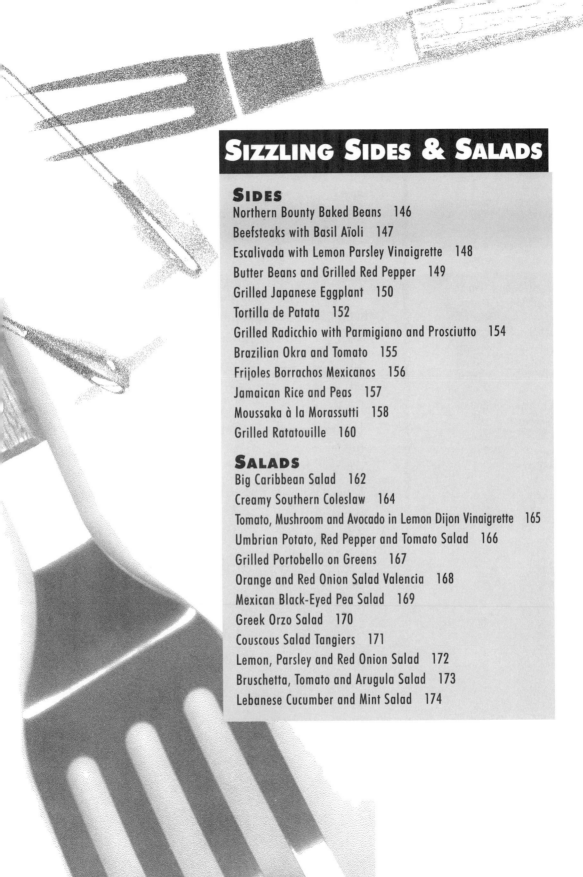

SIZZLING SIDES & SALADS

SIDES

Northern Bounty Baked Beans   146
Beefsteaks with Basil Aïoli   147
Escalivada with Lemon Parsley Vinaigrette   148
Butter Beans and Grilled Red Pepper   149
Grilled Japanese Eggplant   150
Tortilla de Patata   152
Grilled Radicchio with Parmigiano and Prosciutto   154
Brazilian Okra and Tomato   155
Frijoles Borrachos Mexicanos   156
Jamaican Rice and Peas   157
Moussaka à la Morassutti   158
Grilled Ratatouille   160

SALADS

Big Caribbean Salad   162
Creamy Southern Coleslaw   164
Tomato, Mushroom and Avocado in Lemon Dijon Vinaigrette   165
Umbrian Potato, Red Pepper and Tomato Salad   166
Grilled Portobello on Greens   167
Orange and Red Onion Salad Valencia   168
Mexican Black-Eyed Pea Salad   169
Greek Orzo Salad   170
Couscous Salad Tangiers   171
Lemon, Parsley and Red Onion Salad   172
Bruschetta, Tomato and Arugula Salad   173
Lebanese Cucumber and Mint Salad   174

Northern Bounty Baked Beans

Serves 10 to 12

Baked beans — real baked beans — make one of the best partners with grilled fare. The finest ever were served up at the first Northern Bounty, a now bi-annual food conference organized by Cuisine Canada, the national organization that keeps the Canadian culinary scene in sharp focus. These are Calgary cowboy-style baked beans, slow-cooked with salt pork, molasses and pure maple syrup. These are simply the best — there's nothing better with ribs, creamy coleslaw and corn.

Bean pot or heavy casserole with lid

4 cups	dried white navy beans	1 L
10 cups	cold water	2.5 L
1 lb	salt pork, sliced	500 g
2	onions, minced	2
1/2 cup	tomato paste	125 mL
1/2 cup	brown sugar	125 mL
1/2 cup	pure maple syrup	125 mL
1 tbsp	dry mustard	15 mL
1/3 cup	fancy molasses	75 mL

1. Place beans in a colander; wash thoroughly and remove any stones. Place in a large pot with cold water. Soak overnight.

2. Preheat oven to 325° F (160° C). Place beans over high heat; bring to a boil. Reduce heat; simmer gently, covered, for 30 minutes or until tender.

3. Line the inside of bean pot or casserole with salt pork. Set aside.

4. Add onions, tomato paste, brown sugar, maple syrup, mustard and molasses to beans. Stir to blend well. Pour carefully into pork-lined bean pot. Cover; bake, stirring occasionally, in preheated oven for 4 to 4 1/2 hours or until beans are tender and sauce has thickened. Add water if necessary. Remove from heat; discard pork slices before serving.

Beefsteaks with Basil Aïoli

Serves 4

This is a WOW! dish — pure and simple. There is nothing better than grilled beefsteak tomatoes drizzled with home-made garlic mayo and a handful of fresh chopped basil.

A wonderful accompaniment to grilled steak, this recipe is easily doubled.

2	large egg yolks	2
4	cloves garlic, minced	4
2 tbsp	fresh lemon juice	25 mL
1/2 tsp	coarse salt	2 mL
1/4 tsp	white pepper	1 mL
3/4 cup	extra virgin olive oil	175 mL
1/2 cup	chopped fresh basil	125 mL
2	large ripe beefsteak tomatoes, cut in half crosswise	2
	Olive oil	
	Salt and freshly ground black pepper	
	Fresh basil leaves for garnish	

1. In a food processor or blender, combine egg yolks, garlic, lemon juice, salt and white pepper. With motor running, slowly drizzle in olive oil. Continue to blend until the mixture becomes creamy.

2. Transfer mixture to a bowl; fold in basil. If not using immediately, cover and refrigerate. Remove aïoli from refrigerator 30 minutes before using.

3. Preheat grill to medium. Brush cut side of tomatoes with olive oil. Place on grill, cut-side down. Close the lid; grill for 3 minutes per side.

4. Using tongs, transfer tomatoes to a serving platter. Season with salt and pepper. Crown each tomato half with a dollop of aïoli. Garnish with fresh basil leaves. Serve immediately.

Escalivada with Lemon Parsley Vinaigrette

Serves 4 to 6

Escalivada refers to roasted vegetables in Spain where an oven-roasted version of this dish is a very popular *tapas* item. Grilling the eggplant, peppers and zucchini gives them additional appeal. It's wonderful with lots of crusty bread to mop up the juices.

Slide a couple of water-soaked toothpicks through the sliced onion to keep in place on the grill.

Preheat grill to medium-high

1	small eggplant, trimmed and sliced crosswise	1
1	red bell pepper	1
1	green bell pepper	1
1	medium red onion, peeled and cut into wedges	1
1	zucchini, sliced lengthwise	1
	Olive oil	
3 tbsp	extra virgin olive oil	45 mL
1/3 cup	fresh lemon juice	75 mL
2 tbsp	chopped fresh parsley	25 mL
1 tbsp	chopped fresh thyme	15 mL
	Salt and freshly ground black pepper	

1. Brush eggplant, red pepper, green pepper, red onion and zucchini with a little olive oil. Place skin-side down on grill. Cook vegetables for 6 to 15 minutes or until tender and lightly charred, turning and brushing with olive oil.

2. Using tongs, transfer eggplant, onion and zucchini to a serving platter. Transfer peppers to a cutting board; let cool. When ready to handle, halve and seed peppers. Cut into quarters; transfer to platter.

3. In a small bowl, whisk together olive oil, lemon juice, parsley, thyme, salt and pepper. Pour over grilled vegetables. Serve immediately.

Butter Beans and Grilled Red Pepper

Serves 6 to 8

This recipe combines the soft sweetness of beans with the pungency of grilled red peppers and chunks of tomato.

Butter beans are known as dried lima beans in the American South.

Just about any large bean, or assortment of beans, may be substituted for butter beans in this recipe.

3	red bell peppers, grilled, seeded and cut into strips	3
1	large white onion, peeled, halved and thinly sliced	1
1	clove garlic, minced	1
3	cans (each 19 oz [540 mL]) butter beans, rinsed and drained	3
2 cups	canned Italian plum tomatoes, drained, seeded and chopped	500 mL
1/2 cup	chopped flat leaf parsley	125 mL
3 tbsp	extra virgin olive oil	45 mL
1/4 cup	fresh lemon juice	50 mL
1 tsp	finely grated lemon zest	5 mL
	Salt and freshly ground black pepper, to taste	

1. In a large bowl, combine red pepper, onion, garlic, beans, tomatoes and parsley. Toss to combine well.

2. In a small bowl, whisk together olive oil, lemon juice, lemon zest, salt and pepper. Pour over bean mixture; stir to combine. Cover bowl with plastic wrap; let stand for 30 minutes at room temperature. Serve.

Grilled Japanese Eggplant

Serves 4

Because the slender purple (or sometimes white) Japanese eggplant has far fewer seeds and no bitter quality, it is well-suited to a quick seasoning and a fast grilling.

This is a lovely side dish to serve with a selection of Asian-inspired entrées.

Vary this recipe by substituting or adding portobello mushrooms.

Look for both white and black sesame seeds in Asian markets, Indian markets or specialty food shops.

Large shallow glass or ceramic baking dish

4	Japanese eggplants, sliced in half lengthwise, stems intact	4
1/4 cup	fresh lime juice	50 mL
2 tsp	white sesame seeds	10 mL
1 tsp	black sesame seeds	5 mL
1/4 cup	light soya sauce	50 mL
1/4 cup	*mirin* (rice wine) *or* sherry	50 mL
2 tbsp	sesame oil	25 mL
1 tsp	hot chili sauce (or to taste)	5 mL
1/4 tsp	freshly ground black pepper	2 mL
1 tbsp	minced ginger root	15 mL
2 tbsp	vegetable oil	25 mL
3	cloves garlic, minced	3
8 cups	spinach leaves, rinsed and dried	2 L
1/4 cup	chopped fresh chives	50 mL

1. Place eggplant cut-side up on a plate. Pour lime juice over; rub into eggplant.

2. In a small heavy skillet over medium heat, toast white and black sesame seeds for 2 to 5 minutes or until fragrant and slightly colored. Remove from heat; cool.

3. In a small bowl, combine soya sauce, *mirin*, sesame oil, chili sauce, pepper and ginger. In a skillet over medium heat, warm oil. Add garlic and cook for 1 minute. Add soya sauce mixture; stir to combine well. Pour into baking dish.

4. Place eggplant cut-side down in marinade. Let sit at least 30 minutes. Cover and refrigerate if marinating longer.

5. Preheat grill to medium. Using tongs, transfer eggplant to grill. Cook for 3 to 4 minutes per side or until tender and soft.

6. Arrange spinach leaves on serving platter; drizzle with remaining marinade. Arrange eggplant over spinach. Sprinkle with chives and toasted sesame seeds. Serve immediately.

Tortilla de Patata

Serves 4

The Spaniards take their *tortilla de patata* very seriously, perhaps because it is such a satisfying, versatile preparation that is as welcome at breakfast as it is at lunch, dinner or the witching hour. This simply delicious potato omelet is nothing like a conventional omelet — except, of course, for the fact that it combines eggs with other ingredients and is cooked in a skillet. Here, olive oil reigns supreme. It is used in considerable quantity in this recipe but, once you taste the results, you won't have it any other way. Allow the finished dish to sit and cool to room temperature before enjoying with a big earthy Spanish rioja.

If you have one, use a 9-inch (22.5 cm) cast iron pan to prepare the tortilla.

1	onion, finely chopped	1
4	medium baking potatoes, peeled and cut into 1/8-inch (2 mm) thick slices	4
3/4 cup	olive oil, preferably Spanish	175 mL
1/2 tsp	salt	2 mL
1/2 tsp	freshly ground black pepper	2 mL
5	large eggs	5
	Salt, to taste	

1. In a large bowl, combine onion and potatoes. Toss to combine well.

2. In a heavy skillet, heat oil over medium-high heat. Add potato mixture in layers, adding salt and pepper to each layer, until all potatoes and onion are stacked.

3. Reduce heat to medium-low. Cook potatoes, turning often, for 15 to 20 minutes or until tender, being careful not to brown. Remove potatoes to a paper towel-lined plate. Drain, patting with more paper towels.

4. In a bowl, lightly beat eggs with salt. Stir in potatoes; blend well. Let mixture sit at room temperature for about 10 minutes.

5. Pour cooking oil into a bowl. Wipe skillet clean; replace 1 tbsp (15 mL) cooking oil to skillet. Place over medium heat. When oil is hot, add potato mixture. Cook, shaking skillet occasionally, for about 4 minutes or until tortilla is brown on bottom.

6. Place a large plate or pizza pan upside down over skillet. Flip tortilla out to turn over; slip back into skillet. Cook, pressing down and shaking skillet, for about 4 minutes.

7. Transfer to a plate. Serve warm or at room temperature, cut into wedges.

Grilled Radicchio with Parmigiano and Prosciutto

Serves 4

Although it is usually enjoyed fresh, brilliantly colored radicchio has the sturdiness required to withstand the heat of the grill. After a light grilling, radicchio really becomes a whole other creature, its natural bitterness balanced and tempered by the smoke and flame.

Be sure to cut the radicchio lengthwise into quarters, leaving the core intact to hold the leaves together. This method also works well with Romaine lettuce and endive.

Preheat grill to medium-high

2	heads radicchio, rinsed and quartered	2
1/2 cup	extra virgin olive oil	125 mL
1/2 tsp	salt	2 mL
1/2 tsp	freshly ground black pepper	2 mL
1/4 cup	balsamic vinegar	50 mL
4 oz	Parmigiano-Reggiano cheese, thinly sliced	125 g
8	slices prosciutto	8

1. Brush radicchio quarters lightly with half the olive oil. Sprinkle with salt and pepper. Place on grill, slightly away from direct heat. Grill for 1 to 2 minutes per side or until leaves begin to darken and wilt.

2. Place radicchio on a serving platter. Drizzle with balsamic vinegar and remaining olive oil. Top with Parmigiano-Reggiano and prosciutto. Serve immediately.

Brazilian Okra and Tomato

Serves 4 to 6

The Brazilians have a thing for — and a way with — okra. One of their favorite dishes combines fresh okra, tomatoes, onion and garlic. A quick, simple and impressive dish, this is wonderful served alongside grilled jumbo shrimp.

When handling hot chili peppers, wear rubber gloves and avoid any contact with your face.

1/4 cup	olive oil	50 mL
1	large onion, chopped	1
3	cloves garlic, finely chopped	3
1	hot chili pepper, finely chopped	1
1	can (28 oz [796 mL]) whole plum tomatoes, peeled and roughly chopped, with juice	1
1 tsp	granulated sugar	5 mL
1 lb	fresh okra, trimmed and sliced	500 g
	Salt and freshly ground black pepper, to taste	
	Cooked rice	
	Chopped fresh coriander	

1. In a large skillet, heat oil over medium heat. Add onion and cook, stirring often, for 5 minutes or until softened. Add garlic and chili; cook for 5 minutes.

2. Add tomatoes, 1/2 cup (125 mL) of their juice and sugar. Bring to a simmer; add okra. Stir gently to combine well. Cover; simmer for 10 to 15 minutes or until okra is tender. Season to taste with salt and pepper. If sauce is too thick, add more tomato juice.

3. Pour mixture over cooked rice. Sprinkle with chopped coriander. Serve immediately.

Frijoles Borrachos Mexicanos

Serves 8

Borrachos means "drunken" in Spanish and, in this recipe, refers to the fact that both tequila and beer lend their special qualities to the humble pinto bean. Very good with warmed tortillas or as a side dish with Mexican-style grilled fish.

Pinto is Spanish for "painted" — an apt description for these beans, which feature streaks of reddish-brown. Along with pink beans, these are the beans most commonly used in the making of refried beans.

Look for cans of chipotle chili peppers (smoked jalapeños) in the international section of large supermarkets or in Mexican or Latin American markets.

1 lb	dried pinto beans	500 g
1 1/2 cups	Mexican beer	375 mL
5 cups	water	1.25 L
2	chipotle chili peppers, seeded and finely chopped	2
1/2 cup	tequila	125 mL
4	cloves garlic, minced	4
1 tsp	cumin seeds, toasted	5 mL
2 tbsp	vegetable oil	25 mL
1	onion, chopped	1
2	cloves garlic, minced	2
4	tomatoes (fresh or canned), chopped	4
2	fresh jalapeños, seeded and chopped	2
	Salt and freshly ground black pepper, to taste	
1 cup	chopped fresh coriander	250 mL

1. In a colander rinse pinto beans, discarding any stones. Transfer beans to a large pot. Add beer, water, chipotles, garlic and cumin seeds. Bring to a boil; reduce heat. Cover; simmer gently for 1 to 1 1/2 hours or until tender.

2. Meanwhile, heat oil in a skillet over medium heat. Add onion and garlic; cook for 5 minutes or until softened. Add tomatoes, jalapeños, salt and pepper. Simmer, stirring occasionally, for 5 minutes or until thickened. Remove from heat.

3. When beans are done, stir in tomato mixture and tequila; simmer for 5 to 10 minutes. Remove from heat and stir in coriander. Serve immediately.

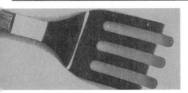

Jamaican Rice and Peas

Serves 6

I like this easy recipe for traditional island-style rice and peas because you can combine all the ingredients in one saucepan ahead of time and forget about it until an hour or so before cooking.

Pigeon peas are also called congo peas and are readily available in cans.

Creamed coconut is sold in blocks, usually wrapped in coated paper. Look for it in the international section of large supermarkets or in West Indian, Indian or Asian markets.

1 1/4 cups	long grain rice	300 mL
1 tsp	salt	5 mL
1	can (14 oz [398 mL]) pigeon peas or kidney beans, drained	1
1/3 cup	chopped creamed coconut	75 mL
1 tbsp	chopped fresh thyme	15 mL
2 1/4 cups	water	550 mL
4	green onions, chopped	4

1. In a large saucepan over medium heat, combine rice, salt, peas, coconut, thyme and water; bring to a boil. Cover, reduce heat and simmer for 15 minutes or until rice is cooked.

2. Remove from heat; let stand for 5 to 10 minutes. Stir in chopped onions. Serve immediately.

Moussaka à la Morassutti

Serves 6 to 8

When I told my friend Eddie Morassutti that I was working on a book devoted to grilling, he produced this really great recipe — a sort of Italian moussaka — which he devised when his garden presented him with an abundance of lovely purple eggplant. *Bravo Eddie!*

Preheat oven to 375° F (190° C)
Preheat grill to medium-high
13- by 9-inch (3 L) baking dish, lightly greased

3	medium eggplants, trimmed and sliced	3
1 tbsp	salt	15 mL
1/3 cup	olive oil	75 mL
2 tbsp	olive oil	25 mL
1	large onion, chopped	1
1/2 cup	chopped fresh parsley	125 mL
1/3 cup	dry white wine	75 mL
3	tomatoes, chopped	3
	Salt and freshly ground black pepper, to taste	
3/4 tsp	ground cinnamon	4 mL
1	can (19 oz [540 mL]) lentils	1
1/4 cup	grated Parmigiano-Reggiano	50 mL
1/4 cup	grated Romano cheese	50 mL
1/4 cup	unsalted butter	50 mL
3 tbsp	all-purpose flour	45 mL
2 cups	milk	500 mL
1/2 tsp	salt	2 mL
1/2 tsp	white pepper	2 mL
1 1/4 cups	ricotta cheese	300 mL
2	eggs	2
1/2 tsp	freshly grated nutmeg	2 mL

1. Place sliced eggplant in a colander set on a plate; sprinkle with salt. Drain for a few minutes. Pat eggplant dry with paper towels. Brush with olive oil; place on grill. Cook, turning once or twice, for 5 minutes per side or until softened and charred in places. Set aside.

2. In a skillet heat olive oil over medium heat. Add onion and cook, stirring occasionally, for 10 minutes or until soft and lightly browned. Stir in parsley, white wine, tomatoes, salt, pepper and cinnamon. Cook for 10 minutes or until thick. Add lentils; mix to combine well. Remove from heat.

3. Cover bottom of baking dish with half the eggplant slices. Add half the Parmigiano-Reggiano and half the Romano cheese. Top with half tomato mixture. Repeat with remaining eggplant, cheese and tomato mixture. Set aside.

4. In a saucepan heat butter over medium heat. Using a whisk, blend in flour; cook for 5 minutes. Add milk gradually, stirring with the whisk constantly. Increase heat to medium-high; bring to a boil, stirring constantly. Boil for 1 minute or until thickened. Stir in salt and white pepper. Remove from heat; set aside to cool slightly.

5. In a bowl combine ricotta cheese, eggs and nutmeg; whisk thoroughly. Stir in white sauce.

6. Pour topping over eggplant; smooth evenly with a spatula. Bake in preheated oven for 45 to 50 minutes or until filling is bubbling and top is golden brown. Allow to sit for 15 minutes before serving.

Grilled Ratatouille

Serves 4 to 6

Here it is — the solution to the annual surfeit of tomatoes, zucchinis and peppers happily endured by many home gardeners. I'm sure the folk in Provence would approve of this contemporary version of their much-revered summer classic.

Preheat lightly oiled grill to medium-high

1/2 cup	extra virgin olive oil	125 mL
3 tbsp	balsamic vinegar	45 mL
1/2 tsp	coarse salt	2 mL
1/2 tsp	freshly ground black pepper	2 mL
1	red bell pepper, seeded and cut into strips	1
1	yellow bell pepper, seeded and cut into strips	1
1	small eggplant, sliced crosswise	1
1	large red onion, thickly sliced	1
1	green zucchini, halved then quartered lengthwise	1
1	yellow zucchini, halved then quartered lengthwise	1
1 1/2 lbs	small ripe tomatoes, halved	750 g
2	heads garlic, tops trimmed	2
2 tbsp	chopped fresh marjoram	25 mL

1. In a small bowl, combine olive oil, balsamic vinegar, salt and pepper. Place red pepper, yellow pepper, eggplant, red onion, green zucchini, yellow zucchini and tomatoes on a platter. Brush with olive oil mixture.

2. Brush garlic heads with a little olive oil. Grill, not quite over direct heat, for 25 minutes or until lightly browned and soft, turning every 10 minutes or so. Remove from grill; allow to cool before peeling.

3. Grill peppers for 8 to 10 minutes or until lightly charred, turning frequently. Transfer to a serving platter. Place eggplant, onion and zucchini on grill. Cook for 8 to 10 minutes or until lightly charred in places and softened. Transfer to serving platter.

Recipe continues nxt page...

ORANGE AND RED ONION SALAD VALENCIA (PAGE 168) ➤

4. Place tomatoes on grill cut-side down. Cook, turning once, for 3 to 5 minutes or until slightly charred. Transfer to serving platter.

5. Add peeled garlic to platter. Drizzle with remaining olive oil mixture. Sprinkle with fresh marjoram. Serve immediately or at room temperature.

≺ Grand Marnier Grilled Oranges (Page 179)

Big Caribbean Salad

Serves 10 to 12

Really big and really good. Reserve this fabulous preparation for when you invite a big crowd over for a mess of jerk chicken or pork — it makes a lot!

SALAD

1	jicama, sliced into matchsticks	1
4	oranges, peeled, pith removed and sectioned	4
1	large red onion, thinly sliced	1
1/2 cup	fresh mint leaves	125 mL
1/2 cup	fresh basil leaves	125 mL
2	green bananas, boiled for 15 minutes in salted water, cut into 1-inch (2.5 cm) slices	2
Half	bunch watercress, washed and stemmed	Half
1	stalk celery, finely chopped	1
1	ripe avocado, cubed	1
1	ripe papaya, cubed	1
1	ripe mango, cubed	1
1	bunch spinach, washed and dried	1
1	small head romaine lettuce, washed, dried and cut into strips	1
1	red bell pepper, thinly sliced	1
1	small head radicchio, washed, dried and torn	1
Half	English cucumber, chopped	Half
1	large carrot, grated	1
3	green onions, finely chopped	3
1 cup	roasted unsalted peanuts	250 mL

DRESSING

1/4 to 1/2 cup	extra virgin olive oil	50 to 125 mL
2 tbsp	sesame oil	25 mL
3 to 4 tbsp	light soya sauce	45 to 50 mL
6 tbsp	fresh lime juice	90 mL
1 tbsp	grated lemon zest	15 mL
1/4 cup	Asian fish sauce *or* Worcestershire sauce	50 mL
2 tbsp	liquid honey	25 mL
1 tsp	Chinese chili sauce	5 mL
1/4 cup	chopped fresh basil	50 mL
	Salt and freshly ground black pepper, to taste	

1. In a very large bowl, combine jicama, oranges, red onion, mint, basil, green bananas, watercress, celery, avocado, papaya, mango, spinach, romaine lettuce, red bell pepper, radicchio, cucumber, carrot, green onions and peanuts.

2. In another bowl, whisk together olive oil, sesame oil, soya sauce, lime juice, lemon zest, fish sauce, honey, chili sauce, basil, salt and pepper. When ready to serve, pour dressing over salad ingredients; toss gently. Serve immediately.

Creamy Southern Coleslaw

Serves 8 to 10

When I was in New Orleans, I tasted some of the best coleslaw ever at a small, family-run restaurant, famous for its chicken, ribs and deep-fried okra. Just about everybody in that restaurant ordered the coleslaw with their main course. I followed their lead and was very glad I did — it was perfect, and it tasted like this.

1/3 cup	mayonnaise	75 mL
2 tbsp	mustard	25 mL
2 tbsp	olive oil	25 mL
2 tbsp	white vinegar	25 mL
1 tbsp	granulated sugar	15 mL
1 tsp	hot sauce	5 mL
1 tsp	salt	5 mL
	Juice of 1 lemon	
	Freshly ground black pepper, to taste	
2	large carrots, shredded	2
2	white onions, thinly sliced	2
2	green bell peppers, seeded and thinly sliced	2
1	medium head green cabbage, cored and shredded	1

1. In a bowl whisk together mayonnaise and mustard. Add olive oil in a thin stream, whisking until thickened. Whisk in vinegar, sugar, hot sauce and salt. Stir in lemon juice. Season to taste with pepper.

2. In a large bowl, combine carrots, onions, peppers and cabbage. Pour dressing over; toss to coat well. Refrigerate for 1 hour before serving.

Tomato, Mushroom and Avocado in Lemon Dijon Vinaigrette

Serves 4 to 6

I have been making this delightful little salad for many years. The Lemon Dijon Vinaigrette with which the vegetables are dressed here has become my "house" dressing. It is the classic dressing for a simple salad of very fresh greens.

1/4 cup	extra virgin olive oil	50 mL
2 tbsp	fresh lemon juice	25 mL
1 tbsp	Dijon mustard	15 mL
1 tsp	granulated sugar	5 mL
1 tsp	salt	5 mL
	Freshly ground black pepper, to taste	
2 cups	ripe cherry tomatoes, halved	500 mL
2 cups	white button mushrooms, halved	500 mL
1	large ripe avocado, chopped	1
1/4 cup	chopped fresh flat leaf parsley	50 mL

1. In a large bowl, whisk together oil and lemon juice. Whisk in Dijon mustard, sugar, salt and black pepper. Adjust seasoning to taste.

2. Add cherry tomatoes, mushrooms, avocado and parsley; toss gently to coat. Allow to sit for 30 minutes at room temperature before serving.

Umbrian Potato, Red Pepper and Tomato Salad

Serves 4 to 6

Here is a dish I created in Italy's Umbria region one afternoon with some ingredients that happened to be on hand. There were a couple of huge, freshly dug potatoes, a big red pepper, an onion, a handful of ripe plum tomatoes and some wonderful, unsmoked, thick-cut bacon. The word "salad" may not really do this substantial dish justice. Whatever you choose to call it, it's delicious and, incidentally, makes an excellent brunch served with fried eggs.

2	large baking potatoes, peeled and quartered	2
3 tbsp	olive oil	45 mL
3 or 4	slices thick bacon, chopped	3 or 4
1	onion, sliced	1
1	red bell pepper, sliced	1
5 or 6	plum tomatoes, chopped	5 or 6
	Salt and freshly ground black pepper, to taste	

1. In a saucepan cook potatoes in boiling water for 12 minutes or until tender when pierced with a knife. Drain. When cool enough to handle, chop into rough chunks. Set aside.

2. In a large skillet, heat oil over medium heat. Add bacon; cook for 5 minutes or until it starts to brown. (If there is more fat at this point than you want, drain some off.) Add sliced onion and red pepper; cook stirring occasionally, for 10 minutes, or until onion is translucent and pepper is softened.

3. Stir in tomatoes and potatoes; cook stirring occasionally, for 10 minutes or until tomatoes break down and mixture is well combined. Season to taste with salt and pepper. Serve immediately.

Grilled Portobello on Greens

Serves 4

"Steaks for vegetarians!" is how a friend of mine describes huge, meaty, grilled portobello mushrooms. The first time I enjoyed a grilled portobello was in an Italian restaurant in New York City. It had been brushed liberally with olive oil, treated to salt and black pepper, grilled and slapped on the plate with not so much as a sprig of parsley to enhance it. Just as well; it was so massive it covered the entire plate. It was delicious. This salad combines the smokiness of grilled portobellos with fresh greens in a big-tasting balsamic vinaigrette.

If portobellos are not available, try grilling an assortment of mushrooms tossed with a little olive oil. If they are particularly small you might want to use a grill basket to keep them from falling through the grate.

Preheat grill to medium-high, lightly greased

2 tbsp	balsamic vinegar	25 mL
1 tbsp	chopped fresh oregano	15 mL
1	clove garlic, minced	1
1/2 tsp	granulated sugar	2 mL
1/3 cup	extra virgin olive oil	75 mL
	Salt and freshly ground black pepper, to taste	
2 lbs	portobello mushrooms, stems removed	1 kg
2 to 3 tbsp	extra virgin olive oil	25 to 45 mL
1/2 tsp	coarse salt	2 mL
6 cups	mixed salad greens	1.5 L
2 oz	Parmigiano-Reggiano, shaved	60 g

1. In a small bowl, combine balsamic vinegar, oregano, garlic and sugar. Whisk together until well blended. Add olive oil in a steady stream, whisking until well combined. Season to taste with salt and pepper. Set aside.

2. In a bowl toss portobello caps with olive oil and coarse salt. Place on grill; close lid and grill for 15 minutes, turning frequently, or until edges are a little crispy and mushrooms are tender.

3. Line 4 plates with salad greens. Slice mushrooms fairly thickly; arrange on greens. Drizzle with vinaigrette; top with Parmigiano-Reggiano. Serve immediately.

Orange and Red Onion
Salad Valencia

Serves 6

Slices of juicy navel oranges tossed with crisp red onion makes for a really refreshing combination, especially when fresh mint is added. This is lovely with many spicy dishes as it has a cooling quality. If the oranges have been refrigerated, allow them to sit for an hour or so at room temperature before making the salad; they should be cool but not cold.

6	seedless navel oranges, peeled, pith removed and cut into 1/4-inch (5 mm) slices	6
1	large red onion, halved and very thinly sliced	1
2 tbsp	extra virgin olive oil	25 mL
1/2 tsp	salt	2 mL
1 tbsp	fresh lemon juice	15 mL
8	fresh mint leaves, cut into thin strips	8

1. In a large bowl, combine oranges and onion. Add olive oil, salt, lemon juice and mint; toss to coat well. Let sit for a few minutes before serving.

Mexican Black-Eyed Pea Salad

Serves 6

Here is a breezy simple salad that works wonderfully well with any Southern-styled barbecue fare. Be sure to allow for extra "sitting" time so the flavors develop fully.

When handling chilies, wear rubber gloves and avoid contact with your face.

1/2 cup	extra virgin olive oil	125 mL
1/4 cup	red wine vinegar	50 mL
1 tsp	salt	5 mL
1/2 tsp	freshly ground black pepper	2 mL
2	cloves garlic, minced	2
2	stalks celery, finely chopped	2
1	large red onion, finely chopped	1
1	green bell pepper, finely chopped	1
2	jalapeño peppers, seeded and finely chopped	2
4 cups	black-eyed peas, cooked and drained (use canned if you wish)	1 L

1. In a small bowl, combine olive oil, vinegar, salt, pepper and garlic. Whisk together well.

2. In a large bowl, combine celery, onion, green pepper, jalapeño peppers and black-eyed peas. Pour dressing over vegetables; stir to combine well. Cover; refrigerate for 2 hours, stirring occasionally. (May be made 1 day ahead.) Let stand at room temperature for 1 hour before serving.

Greek Orzo Salad

Serves 4 to 6

I love this simple salad. It combines all the best things about a traditional Greek salad, with cooked orzo — the plump, rice-shaped pasta (it means 'barley' in Italian) — that is favored by Greeks. This salad makes a nice accompaniment to souvlaki or grilled lamb.

2 tsp	chopped fresh dill	10 mL
2	cloves garlic, minced	2
1/4 cup	extra virgin olive oil	50 mL
3 tbsp	fresh lemon juice	45 mL
2 tbsp	red wine vinegar	25 mL
	Salt and freshly ground black pepper, to taste	
1 cup	orzo (rice-shaped pasta)	250 mL
4	fresh plum tomatoes, chopped	4
1	small English cucumber, unpeeled and chopped	1
3	green onions, chopped	3
8 oz	feta cheese, crumbled	250 g
1	head romaine lettuce, rinsed, dried and shredded	1

1. In a small bowl, combine dill, garlic, olive oil, lemon juice and red wine vinegar. Whisk to blend well. Season to taste with salt and pepper.

2. In a pot of boiling salted water, cook orzo according to package directions or until tender but firm (do not overcook). Drain; rinse briefly under cold running water. Drain thoroughly.

3. Transfer orzo to a serving bowl. Add tomatoes, cucumber, green onions and feta cheese. Pour dressing over; toss to combine well. To serve, arrange shredded romaine lettuce on serving plates. Top with orzo/vegetable mixture.

Couscous Salad Tangiers

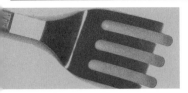

Serves 4

Couscous is a staple of the North African diet, where the cooked semolina is used in many traditional dishes. Look for the "quick-cook" (actually pre-cooked) couscous that is readily available in many large supermarkets or Middle Eastern markets. Adjust the amount of cayenne according to your taste.

1 tbsp	vegetable oil	15 mL
1 cup	slivered almonds	250 mL
1	onion, chopped	1
1	small red bell pepper, chopped	1
2	green onions, chopped	2
2 cups	fresh orange juice	500 mL
2	cinnamon sticks, broken	2
1/4 tsp	turmeric	1 mL
1/4 tsp	cayenne	1 mL
	Salt and freshly ground black pepper, to taste	
2 cups	quick-cook couscous	500 mL
1/4 cup	golden raisins	50 mL
1/2 cup	chopped fresh coriander	125 mL

1. In a large skillet, heat oil over medium-high heat. Add almonds; toast for 3 minutes, shaking pan frequently, or until golden.

2. Stir in chopped onion, red pepper and green onions. Reduce heat to medium; cook, stirring frequently, for 6 minutes, or until vegetables are tender and browned. Stir in orange juice. Add broken cinnamon sticks, turmeric, cayenne, salt and pepper.

3. Bring mixture to a boil. Stir in couscous and raisins. Remove from heat, cover skillet and let sit for 5 minutes or until liquid is absorbed. Using a large fork, fluff grains. Add coriander; fluff gently. Serve immediately.

Lemon, Parsley and Red Onion Salad

Serves 4

This is a unique preparation that works extremely well with rich fish such as salmon, tuna or swordfish. Take care to remove all of the lemon's bitter white pith; otherwise, it will affect the flavor of the finished dish.

4	lemons, peel and pith removed	4
3	red onions, finely chopped	3
1/2 cup	chopped flat leaf parsley	125 mL
4	fresh plum tomatoes, diced	4
2 tbsp	extra virgin olive oil	25 mL
	Salt and freshly ground black pepper, to taste	

1. On a cutting board with a groove (to collect juice), slice lemons into circles. Stack lemon slices and cut in half, then quarters, then eighths.

2. Transfer diced lemons and collected juice into a large bowl. Add onions, parsley, tomatoes and oil; toss to coat well. Season to taste with salt and pepper. Let stand for a few minutes before serving.

Bruschetta, Tomato and Arugula Salad

Serves 4 to 6

This is my take on the very old, very revered Tuscan Bread Salad. Use a good rustic Italian bread for this recipe — one sturdy enough to stand up to the grill. Day-old bread is fine.

Preheat grill to medium-high

6	slices white Italian country-style bread	6
	Olive oil	
1 to 2	large cloves garlic, halved	1 to 2
2 tbsp	red wine vinegar	25 mL
1 tbsp	balsamic vinegar	15 mL
	Salt and freshly ground black pepper	
3	cloves garlic, minced	3
1	shallot, minced	1
1/2 cup	extra virgin olive oil	125 mL
3	fresh plum tomatoes, diced	3
Half	English cucumber, unpeeled and diced	Half
1	large red onion, thinly sliced	1
1	bunch arugula, rinsed, dried and torn	1

1. Brush both sides of bread with olive oil. Place on grill; grill for 1 minute per side or until toasted and grill-marked. Cool slightly; rub both sides of bread with garlic halves. Set aside.

2. In a small bowl, whisk together red wine vinegar, balsamic vinegar, salt and pepper. Add minced garlic and shallots; let sit for about 45 minutes. Strain through a sieve into another small bowl; whisk in olive oil.

3. Rip grilled bread into bite-sized pieces. Place in a large serving bowl. Add tomatoes, cucumber, onion and arugula. Add vinaigrette; toss to combine well. Let sit for a few minutes before serving.

Lebanese Cucumber and Mint Salad

Serves 6

There's nothing easier than this ultra-refreshing salad, which combines thick yogurt with very thinly sliced cucumber and masses of fresh mint. It is one of my favorites and wonderful served alongside spicy grilled kebabs.

3 cups	plain yogurt (not low-fat)	750 mL
20	fresh mint leaves	20
2	cloves garlic, peeled	2
1/2 tsp	salt	2 mL
2	large English cucumbers, peeled and thinly sliced	2

1. Over a bowl, place a sieve lined with cheesecloth. Spoon yogurt into sieve; drain for 3 hours. Discard liquid collected in bowl.

2. In a bowl combine mint, garlic and salt. Crush, using a pestle or similar utensil, until mint leaves are mostly disintegrated.

3. Add drained yogurt and the cucumbers. Stir to blend well. Cover; chill for 30 minutes before serving.

SWEETS HEREAFTER

DESSERTS
Bitton Berry Terrine   176
Brown Bread Ice Cream   177
Open-Faced Peach Pie   178
Grand Marnier Grilled Oranges   179
Granita di Caffe con Panna   180
Mexican Fruit Salad   181

DRINKS
Mango Lassi   182
Icy Brazilian "Chocola"   183
Four-Fruit Frappé   184
Lemon Grass Lemonade   185

Bitton Berry Terrine

Serves 4 to 6

Years ago I lived in a small English village called Bitton, which sat directly in between the cities of Bristol and Bath. Down the country road from our very old house lay a pathway that led me, one brilliant summer afternoon, to a seemingly abandoned, never-ending row of blackberry bushes heavy with ripe fruit. What a treasure! My mother and I (and my two daughters) picked and picked, until we had enough for blackberry jam, blackberry tarts and this magnificent summer dessert of jelly and fresh berries.

You will need a lot of fresh berries for this dessert — a total of 6 cups (1.5 L). Use any combination of blackberry, strawberry, raspberry, red currant or blueberry. Save it for a day when summer berries are at their best and you plan to visit a pick-your-own berry farm.

Choose an inexpensive, sweet bubbly for this dessert.

Plan to make this the day before or very early in the day so that the terrine has enough time to set completely.

9- by 5-inch (2 L) baking pan

2 cups	fresh strawberries, stemmed	500 mL
2 cups	fresh raspberries	500 mL
2 cups	mixed berries (see note, at left)	500 mL
2 cups	pink champagne or sparkling wine	500 mL
1/4 cup	granulated sugar	50 mL
2	packets plain gelatin	2
1 tbsp	lemon juice	15 mL
	Unsweetened whipped cream	

1. If strawberries are large, cut in half. In a large mixing bowl, combine strawberries, raspberries and mixed berries. Set aside.

2. In a small saucepan over medium-high heat, bring 1 cup (250 mL) champagne to a simmer. Reduce heat to low; whisk in sugar and gelatin. Remove from heat; whisk until gelatin and sugar are completely dissolved. Stir in lemon juice and remaining champagne. Pour into a large measuring cup; allow to cool.

3. Attractively arrange a layer of fruit on bottom of pan. Carefully add remaining fruit. Pour part of champagne mixture over fruit, reserving about 1 cup (250 mL). Pour reserved liquid back into saucepan; set aside.

4. Cover loaf pan with plastic wrap. Fit a piece of stiff cardboard on top of plastic wrap. Weight top with a couple of cans. Chill terrine in refrigerator for 1 1/2 hours or until set.

5. Reheat reserved wine-gelatin mixture. Remove weights, cardboard and plastic wrap. Pour reheated liquid over terrine. Replace wrap; chill terrine for 3 hours or overnight until completely set.

6. To serve, fill sink with a little hot water. Set loaf pan in it for 15 seconds. Run a knife around edges of pan. Carefully turn terrine onto serving platter. Slice with a sharp knife dipped in hot water. Serve with unsweetened whipped cream.

Brown Bread Ice Cream

Serves 4 to 6

Another very old-fashioned English dessert that no one will believe contains brown bread. A wonderful recipe which doesn't require an ice cream maker.

Use good quality, bakery wholewheat bread for the crumbs.

Preheat oven to 400° F (200° C)
Baking sheet, lightly greased

1/2 cup	fine brown breadcrumbs	125 mL
1/2 cup	packed light brown sugar	125 mL
2 cups	whipping (35%) cream	500 mL
2 tbsp	brandy *or* pure vanilla extract	25 mL
1	large egg white	1

1. In a small bowl, combine breadcrumbs with sugar; toss together until well blended. Spread on prepared baking sheet. Bake in preheated oven, stirring occasionally, for 8 to 10 minutes or until sugar caramelizes and crumbs begin to deepen in color. Remove from oven; let cool. Break up into small bits.

2. In a chilled bowl, whip cream until soft peaks form. Stir in caramelized crumbs and brandy. Pour mixture into a plastic container with lid. Freeze for a few hours until mixture has begun to set around edges and center is mushy.

3. Whisk egg white until just stiff. Remove semi-frozen ice cream from freezer. Beat lightly with an electric mixer (do this right in container) for a few minutes. Fold in egg white with a spoon. Replace lid; return ice cream to freezer until completely frozen.

Open-Faced Peach Pie

Serves 4 to 6

In France this easy one-crust pie, called a *croustade*, is made with all manner of ripe summer fruits — apricots, berries or cherries.

You can vary this recipe by combining half peaches and half plums. If you have a favorite pastry recipe, certainly use it here. Just make sure you have enough for about a 14-inch (35 cm) crust.

Add a little lemon juice to the peaches to keep them from browning.

Large baking sheet

PASTRY

1 1/3 cups	all-purpose flour	325 mL
1/2 cup	butter	125 mL
1 tbsp	granulated sugar	15 mL
Pinch	salt	Pinch

FILLING

1 1/2 lbs	peaches peeled, pitted and thickly sliced	750 g
1/3 cup	granulated sugar	75 mL
1 tbsp	cornstarch	15 mL
1/4 tsp	freshly grated nutmeg	1 mL
2 tbsp	butter	25 mL
1	egg white, beaten	1
	Granulated sugar	
	Whipped cream	

1. In a food processor, combine flour, butter, sugar and salt. Using on/off button, process until mixture resembles fine breadcrumbs. Transfer to a bowl. Add 2 tbsp (25 mL) cold water; mix gently with a fork. If necessary, add more water until dough holds together. Gather into a ball; flatten slightly. Wrap in plastic wrap and chill for about 1 hour.

2. On a lightly floured surface, roll out pastry to a 12-inch (30 cm) circle. Wrap pastry around a rolling pin; transfer to center of baking sheet.

3. Preheat oven to 400° F (200° C). In a bowl combine peaches, sugar, cornstarch and nutmeg. Pile mixture in center of pastry. Dot with butter. Turn up edges of pastry over filling, overlapping pastry as necessary and leaving center of filling uncovered. (Pastry edges should be a little uneven.) Brush off any excess flour. Coat with egg white; sprinkle with a bit of sugar.

4. Bake in top third of oven for 30 to 40 minutes or until pastry is golden brown. Remove from oven; cool slightly. Serve warm with lightly whipped, unsweetened cream.

Grand Marnier Grilled Oranges

Serves 4 to 6

This is one of those "WOW!" desserts — incredibly easy and incredibly good. It was kindly brought to my attention by David Taylor, marketing whiz for Grand Marnier, who urges it be served with quality vanilla ice cream.

Preheat grill or barbecue to medium-high

4 to 6	large navel oranges, peeled, pith removed and cut into 1/2-inch (1 cm) slices	4 to 6
1 cup	Grand Marnier Cordon Rouge (or to taste)	250 mL
	Vanilla ice cream	

1. Place orange slices in a shallow dish. Cover with Grand Marnier. Turn slices over once or twice. Cover with plastic wrap. Chill for at least 1 hour.

2. Grill orange slices, brushing carefully with reserved marinade, for 2 to 4 minutes per side or until caramelized. Serve hot with vanilla ice cream.

Granita di Caffe con Panna

Serves 4 to 6

A slushy for adults, this Italian favorite is refreshing and simple to make. While the hazelnut flavors of Frangelico are particularly compatible with this dessert, any other liqueur may be used.

Serving this granita with biscotti will complete the Italian experience.

2 cups	water	500 mL
1 cup	granulated sugar	250 mL
3/4 cup	strong brewed Italian espresso	175 mL
1 1/4 cups	whipping (35%) cream	300 mL
1 tbsp	granulated sugar	15 mL
1/4 cup	Frangelico (hazelnut liqueur)	50 mL

1. In a heavy-bottomed saucepan, combine water and 1 cup (250 mL) sugar. Bring to a boil, stirring. Reduce heat to medium; cook until sugar is completely dissolved. Remove from heat; stir in espresso. Cool to room temperature. Pour into plastic container and freeze until solid.

2. Remove from freezer. Let stand at room temperature for 1 minute. Transfer to a blender or food processor; blend until slushy. Return to plastic container; freeze for at least 1 hour.

3. One hour before serving, transfer granita to refrigerator to soften slightly.

4. In a chilled bowl, whip cream with 1 tbsp (15 mL) sugar until soft peaks form. In tall serving glasses, alternately layer granita, whipped cream and Frangelico. End with whipped cream and a final drizzle of liqueur. Serve immediately.

Mexican Fruit Salad

Serves 6

Colorful and a joy for melon lovers, this is a lovely fresh-tasting fruit salad that can be made with any number of melon combinations.

3 cups	bite-sized chunks watermelon	750 mL
1 1/2 cups	bite-sized chunks cantaloupe	375 mL
1 1/2 cups	bite-sized chunks crenshaw melon	375 mL
1/4 cup	fresh lime juice	50 mL
1/2 cup	fresh mint leaves, torn	125 mL
1 to 2 tbsp	granulated sugar	15 to 25 mL

1. In a large bowl, stir together watermelon, cantaloupe, crenshaw melon and lime juice. Sprinkle with mint and sugar; stir together.

2. Cover and chill for 30 minutes before serving.

Mango Lassi

Serves 4

Soothing, cooling and a lovely alternative to rich, creamy milkshakes, this classic East Indian beverage is a perfect accompaniment to a spicy appetizer.

Good quality canned mangoes are just fine for this recipe. Be sure to drain well before using.

2 cups	plain yogurt	500 mL
1 1/2 cups	chopped mango	375 mL
2 tbsp	granulated sugar	25 mL
1/4 tsp	ground cardamom	1 mL
8 to 10	ice cubes	8 to 10
	Fresh mint sprigs for garnish	

1. In a blender or food processor, combine yogurt, mango, sugar, cardamom and ice cubes; blend until relatively smooth.

2. Pour into glasses and serve with a sprig of mint.

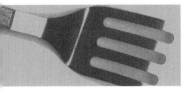

Icy Brazilian 'Chocola'

Serves 4 to 6

A good friend of mine, who spent his formative years in Brazil, introduced me to a number of terrific recipes. This is definitely one of the best — sort of a cross between a beverage and dessert.

3 oz	unsweetened chocolate	90 g
1/4 cup	granulated sugar	50 mL
1 cup	hot strong brewed coffee	250 mL
2 1/2 cups	whole (4%) milk	625 mL
1 cup	whipping (35%) cream	250 mL
1 tbsp	granulated sugar	15 mL
1 1/2 cups	chilled cola	375 mL
	Ice cubes	
	Chocolate shavings or sprinkles	

1. In a bowl set over hot (not boiling) water, melt chocolate. Stir in 1/4 cup (50 mL) sugar until dissolved. Whisk in hot coffee until smooth. Gradually whisk in milk. Continue to cook, stirring, for 10 minutes or until mixture is smooth and heated through. Pour into a pitcher. Cover and chill.

2. In a chilled bowl, whip cream with 1 tbsp (15 mL) sugar until stiff peaks form.

3. Stir cola into chilled chocolate-coffee mixture. Serve over ice with a large dollop of whipped cream and a few chocolate shavings. Alternatively, replace ice cubes with a scoop of vanilla ice cream and serve with long spoons.

Four-Fruit Frappé

Serves 4 to 6

Kids love this as a drinkable dessert — adults love it with a splash of white rum.

Creamed coconut is sold in boxes in the international or baking sections of most supermarkets.

2 cups	ice cubes	500 mL
1 cup	apricot nectar	250 mL
3/4 cup	pineapple juice	175 mL
Half	ripe banana	Half
1/3 cup	whole frozen raspberries (not in syrup)	75 mL
1 tbsp	creamed coconut	15 mL
	Fresh mint sprigs for garnish	

1. In a blender or food processor, combine ice cubes, apricot nectar, pineapple juice, banana, raspberries and creamed coconut. Process until smooth and creamy. Serve in tall chilled glasses with a sprig of mint.

Lemon Grass Lemonade

Serves 4 to 6

I first tasted this incredible drink in a hot and dusty street market in Bangkok. The hint of ginger and wonderful citrus tang make it the most refreshing, satisfying lemonade ever.

Be sure to serve ice cold.

2	stalks lemon grass, trimmed	2
3 cups	water	750 mL
1 cup	granulated sugar	250 mL
1 cup	fresh lemon juice	250 mL
1/2 cup	fresh lime juice	125 mL
1/2 tsp	salt	2 mL
	Ice cubes	

1. Using flat side of a chef's knife, gently bruise lemon grass stalks. Cut into 1/2-inch (1 cm) pieces.

2. In a heavy-bottomed saucepan over medium-high heat, combine lemon grass, water and sugar. Bring to a boil, stirring to dissolve sugar. Reduce heat to medium-low; simmer gently for 15 minutes or until syrupy and fragrant. Pour through a sieve into a large pitcher. Cool to room temperature.

3. Stir in lemon juice, lime juice and salt. Cover with plastic wrap; chill.

4. Before serving, add 10 ice cubes. To serve, pour over more ice into tall glasses.

Index

A

Adobo sauce, about, 29
African red spice paste, 32-33
Aïoli:
  basil, 147
  coriander lemon, 144
Anchovy and herb butter, 45
Annatto seeds, about, 95
Anticuchos, 95
Apricots, dried, sosaties, 130
Argentinian short ribs of beef, 82-83
Asian-flavored pork tenderloin, 98
Australian-style:
  grilled chicken, 119
  spices and herbs, about, 142
Avocado, and tomatillo salsa, 139

B

Bacon:
  back, with maple mustard mop, 96
  and zucchini wrapped scallops, 69
Baked beans, 146
Banquet burger, 92
Barbecue sauces:
  bourbon, 35
  Carolina, 37
  good-for-everything, 34
  mungo mojo rojo, 36
  See also Sauces
Basil, pesto, 54-55
Beans:
  baked, 146
  pinto, Mexican-style, 156
Beef:
  brisket, barbecued, 90-91
  burgers, 92
  short ribs, 82-83
  Singapore satay, 66-67

Beef (continued):
  steak,
    filet mignon, 85
    flank, 88-89
    New York striploin, 84
    sirloin, 93, 95
    T-bone, 94
Beer brats on a bun with sauerkraut, 99
Berberé, 32-33
Berries, terrine, 176
Bistecca alla Florentine, 94
Black peppercorn and garlic butter, 48
Bourbon barbecue sauce, 35
Bratwurst with sauerkraut on a bun, 99
Brazilian-style:
  churrasco, 84
  okra and tomato, 155
Bread:
  about, 124
  bruschetta,, tomato and arugula salad, 173
  toasts for soup, 58-59
Brown bread ice cream, 177
Bruschetta, tomato and arugula salad, 173
Bulgogi:
  about, 86
  sauce, 86-87
Burgers:
  beef, 92
  lamb, 114-15
  tuna, 136
Butter beans, with grilled red pepper, 149
Butters, 40-50
  about, 40
  anchovy and herb, 45
  black peppercorn and garlic, 48
  chive parsley and garlic, 41
  garlic and ginger, 50
  jalapeño lemon and lime, 47
  Lavender Hill, 43

Butters (continued):
    raspberry mustard, 42
    Roquefort cheese, 40
    salsa, 44
    sun-dried tomato and oregano, 46
    tarragon and shallot, 49
    to wrap and chill, 40

C

Cabbage, coleslaw, 164
Canadian banquet burger, 92
Cape Town sosaties, 130
Caribbean salad, 162-63
Carolina barbecue sauce, 37
Chèvre terrine, vegetable and, 76-77
Chicken:
    barbecued Moroccan-style, 128
    breasts,
        Australian-style, 119
        Cuban mojo, 122-23
        with piri-piri sauce, 129
        sosaties, 130
        teriyaki, 126
    roasting, split and grilled, 125
    Singapore satay, 66-67
    soup, tortilla and lime, 60
    thighs,
        Malaysian satay, 120-21
        tikka, 124
    wings, 75
    yakitori, 74
Chilies, about, 28, 78, 107, 155, 169
Chimichurri sauce, 82-83
Chinese baby back ribs, 97
Chipotles:
    about, 25, 29
    paste, 29
Chive parsley and garlic butter, 41
Churrasco, about, 84
Citrus:
    as tenderizer, 16
    trio marinade, 16

Coconut milk:
    about, 66
    pork back ribs, 100-1
Coleslaw, 164
Coriander lemon aïoli, scallops with, 144
Cornmeal, grilled polenta, 64
Corn soup with pesto swirl, 54-55
Couscous salad Tangiers, 171
Cream of watercress soup with nasturtiums,
    56-57
Creamy southern coleslaw, 164
Crème fraîche, 53
Crimson Thai paste, 28
Cubanelle peppers, with lamb loins, 110-11
Cuban-style:
    lobster tails with chipotle mojo, 140
    mojo chicken, 122-23
Cucumber:
    fresh tuna with, 62
    Greek orzo salad, 170
    and mint salad, 174
    soup, 52
    tzatziki, 114-15

D

Desserts:
    Bitton berry terrine, 176
    brown bread ice cream, 177
    four-fruit frappé, 184
    fruit salad, 181
    Grand Marnier grilled oranges, 179
    granita di caffe con panna, 180
    peach pie, 178
Dressing:
    Caribbean, 162-63
    salad, 122-23
Drinks:
    four-fruit frappé, 184
    icy Brazilian 'chocola', 183
    lemon grass lemonade, 185
    mango lassi, 182
Duck, grilled breast of, 131

Dumplings, Southeast Asian, 70-71
Duxelles, about, 85

E

Eggplant:
  Japanese, grilled, 150-51
  moussaka, 158-59
  ratatouille, 160-61
  vegetable and chèvre terrine, 76-77
Eggs, potato omelet, 152-53
Escalivada, with vinaigrette, 148

F

Feta cheese, Greek orzo salad, 170
Filet mignon with duxelles, 85
Fish fillets, grilled, with greens, 137
Five-spice powder, about, 20, 24
Five-spice rub, 24
Four-fruit frappé, 184
Frijoles borrachos Mexicanos, 156
Fruit:
  frappé, 184
  salad, 181

G

Garam masala, about, 17
Garlic:
  and black peppercorn butter, 48
  and ginger butter, 50
  purée, 93
  rub Mexican-style, 23
Ginger root, to juice, 18
Glazes:
  marmalade mustard, 15
  peach chutney, 38
  pepper, pineapple and rum, 39
Grand Marnier grilled oranges, 179
Granita di caffe con panna, 180
Grecian skewered lamb with vegetables, 116-17
Greek Isle-style squid, 141
Greek orzo salad, 170
Green beans, salad Niçoise, 134-35

H

Haddock, grilled, with greens, 137
Halibut, with Brazilian spice, 132
Herbes de Provence, rub, 26
Huachinango with tomatillo and avocado salsa, 139

I

Ice cream:
  brown bread, 177
  granita di caffe con panna, 180
Icy Brazilian 'chocola', 183

J

Jalapeño lemon and lime butter, 47
Jamaican-style:
  jerk pork, 106-7
  rice and peas, 157
Japanese eggplant, grilled, 150-51
Jerk:
  rub, 22
  sugarcane shrimp, 143
Julia's potato and jalapeño quesadillas, 68

K

Kebabs:
  chicken tikka, 124
  Sikh lamb, 112-13
  sosaties, 130
  Turkish grilled lamb, 110-11
Kecap manis, about, 120
Korean bulgogi, 86-87

L

Lamb:
  burgers with mint tzatziki, 114-15
  Grecian skewered, 116-17
  leg of, boned butterflied, Provençal, 108-9
  loins, grilled with peppers, 110-11
  racks, with pomegranate molasses glaze, 118
  Sikh kebab, 112-13
  Singapore satay, 66-67

Lamb (continued):
    tenderloin, on lavosh, 65
Lavosh, about, 65
Lavender Hill butter, 43
Lebanese cucumber and mint salad, 174
Lemon grass:
    about, 21
    lemonade, 185
    marinade, 21
Lemon myrtle shrimp, 142
Lemon(s):
    Dijon vinaigrette, 165
    to juice, 16
    lemon grass lemonade, 185
    marinade, 16
    parsley, tomato and red onion salad, 172
    parsley vinaigrette, 148
Lima beans, with grilled red pepper, 149
Lime(s):
    to juice, 16
    marinade, 16
Lobster tails with chipotle mojo, 140

M
Malaysian chicken satay, 120-21
Mango lassi, 182
Marinades:
    for beef strip loin, 86-87
    bourbon barbecue sauce, 35
    citrus, 16, 122-23
    for flank steak, 88-89
    marmalade mustard, 15
    masala, 17
    mungo mojo rojo, 36
    Polynesian, 19
    Szechwan, 20
    teriyaki ginger, 18
    tikka, 124
    Vietnamese lemon grass, 21
Marmalade, mustard marinade, 15
Masala marinade, 17
Meatballs, in salsa roja, 72-73
Mexican oregano, about, 23, 60

Mexican-style:
    black-eyed pea salad, 169
    fruit salad, 181
    garlic rub, 23
Mint tzatziki, 114-15
Mirin, about, 18
Mobay jerk rub, 22
Mojo sauce, about, 122
Moroccan barbecued chicken, 128
Moussaka à la Morassutti, 158-59
Mungo mojo rojo, 36
Mushrooms, duxelles, 85

O
Okra and tomato, 155
Orange(s):
    Grand Marnier grilled, 179
    to juice, 16
    marinade, 16
    and red onion salad Valencia, 168
Orzo, Greek salad, 170

P
Pacific Rim coconut ribs, 100-1
Pancetta, pizza with porcini, fontina and, 61
Pastes:
    African red spice, 32-33
    all-round, 31
    chipotle, 29
    crimson Thai, 28
    rosemary, lemon and mustard, 30
    smoke and fire, 29
Peach:
    chutney glaze, 38
    pie, 178
Peanut sauce, 66-67
Peas, and rice, 157
Peppers. *See* Chilies; Chipotles; Cubanelle
    peppers; Red bell peppers
Pesce spada alla griglia, 138
Pesto, basil, 54-55
Pickerel, grilled, with greens, 137
Pie, peach, 178

Pigeon peas, and rice, 157
Piri-piri sauce, 129
Pita breads, lamb burgers, 114-15
Pizza, with pancetta, porcini and fontina, 61
Polenta, grilled, 64
Pollo alla diavola, 125
Polynesian marinade, 19
Pomegranate molasses, about, 118
Porcini mushrooms, pancetta and fontina
    with pizza, 61
Pork:
  back ribs,
    Chinese-style, 97
    coconut, 100-1
  loin, pulled, 102-3
  meatballs in salsa roja, 72-73
  Singapore satay, 66-67
  tenderloin,
    Asian flavor, 98
    Jamaican jerk, 106-7
  Vietnamese-style in lettuce, 104-5
Portobello mushrooms, grilled, on greens, 167
Portuguese-style grilled chicken with piri-piri
    sauce, 129
Potato(es):
  and jalapeño quesadillas, 68
  omelet, 152-53
  red pepper and tomato salad, 166
  salad Niçoise, 134-35
Prosciutto, with radicchio, 154
Provençal-style:
  leg of lamb with lavender, 108-9
  rub, 26

Q
Quail with Asian flavors, 127
Quesadillas, potato and jalapeño, 68
Queso fresco, about, 78

R
Rack of lamb, 118
Radicchio, grilled with Parmigiano and
    prosciutto, 154

Raspberry(ies):
  mustard butter, 42
  terrine, 176
Ratatouille, grilled, 160-61
Reader's rainbow trout, 133
Red bell peppers:
  to grill, 53
  grilled with cheese, 78
  pineapple and rum glaze, 39
  soup with crème fraîche, 53
Red chili, rub, 25
Red chili powders, about, 25
Red spice paste, African, 32-33
Rice, and peas, 157
Rice noodles, Vietnamese grilled steak with,
    93
Ricotta cheese, moussaka, 158-59
Roasted vegetables, with vinaigrette, 148
Roquefort butter, 40
Rosemary, lemon and mustard paste, 30
Royal Thai wings, 75
Rubs:
  for beef ribs, 82-83
  crimson Thai paste, 28
  garam masala, 17
  Mexican garlic, 23
  Mobay jerk, 22
  Provençal, 26
  red chili, 25
  Tandoori-style, 27

S
Salads:
  bruschetta, tomato and arugula, 173
  Caribbean, 162-63
  couscous, 171
  creamy southern coleslaw, 164
  cucumber and mint, 174
  Greek orzo, 170
  lemon, parsley, onion and tomato, 172
  Mexican black-eyed pea, 169
  orange and red onion, 168
  portobello on greens, 167

Salads (continued):
tomato, mushroom and avocado, 165
tuna Niçoise, 134-35
Salmon:
with Brazilian spice, 132
with cucumber, 62
Salsa:
butter, 44
tomatillo and avocado, 139
Sambal, tomato, 130
Santa Fe red chili rub, 25
Satay:
Malaysian chicken, 120-21
Singapore, 66-67
Sauces:
bulgogi, 86-87
chimichurri, 82-83
for flank steak, 88-89
peanut, 66-67
piri-piri, 129
See also Barbecue sauces
Scallops:
bacon and zucchini wrapped, 69
with coriander lemon aïoli, 144
with lemon myrtle, 142
Shrimp:
dumplings, 70-71
jerk, 143
Spanish, 63
tiger, with lemon myrtle, 142
Sikh lamb kebab, 112-13
Singapore satay, 66-67
Smoked trout spread, 79
Smoke and fire paste, 29
Snapper:
grilled, with greens, 137
with salsa, 139
Soups, 52-60
cold,
cucumber, 52
grilled red pepper, 53
tomato with basil and toasts, 58-59
corn with pesto swirl, 54-55

Soups (continued):
cream of watercress, 56-57
tortilla and lime, 60
Southeast Asian dumplings, 70-71
Southern pulled pork, 102-3
Souvlaki, about, 116
Soya sauce, about light, 19
Spanish-style:
meatballs in salsa roja, 72-73
shrimp, 63
Spices, tarka technique, 113
Squid, Greek-style, 141
Star anise, about, 24
Starters, 61-79
bacon and zucchini wrapped scallops, 69
chicken wings, 75
grilled lamb on lavosh, 65
grilled peppers with cheese, 78
grilled polenta, 64
meatballs in salsa roja, 72-73
pizza with pancetta, porcini and fontina, 61
potato and jalapeño quesadillas, 68
shrimp dumplings, 70-71
Singapore satay, 66-67
smoked trout spread, 79
Spanish shrimp, 63
tuna with cucumber, 62
vegetable and chèvre terrine, 76-77
yakitori, 74
Strawberries, terrine, 176
Sumatra-style grilled fish with greens, 137
Sun-dried tomato and oregano butter, 46
Swordfish:
with Brazilian spice, 132
grilled, 138
with lemon myrtle, 142
Szechwan-style:
marinade, 20
peppercorns, about, 24

T

Tandoori-style rub, 27
Tarka technique, about, 113

Tarragon and shallot butter, 49
Teriyaki:
    chicken, 126
    ginger marinade, 18
Terrine, Bitton berry, 176
Texas barbecued brisket, 90-91
Thai-style:
    barbecued flank steak, 88-89
    wings, 75
Tikka marinade, 124
Toasts, for tomato soup, 58-59
Tomatillo, and avocado salsa, 139
Tomato(es):
    with basil aïoli, 147
    bruschetta and arugula salad, 173
    Greek orzo salad, 170
    mushroom and avocado salad, 165
    and potato salad, 166
    sambal, 130
    soup with toasts, 58-59
    vegetable and chèvre terrine, 76-77
Tortilla de patata, 152-53
Tortilla(s):
    and lime soup Zocalo, 60
    potato and jalapeño quesadillas, 68
Trout:
    rainbow, 133
    See also Smoked trout
Tuna:
    with Brazilian spice, 132
    burgers, 136
    with cucumber, 62
    to marinate and grill, 62
    salad Niçoise, 134-35
Turkish grilled lamb with peppers, 110-11
Tzatziki, mint, 114-15

U

Umbrian potato, red pepper and tomato
    salad, 166

V

Vegetables:
    and chèvre terrine, 76-77
    Grecian skewered lamb with, 116-17
Vietnamese-style:
    grilled breast of duck, 131
    grilled steak, 93
    lemon grass marinade, 21
    pork in lettuce, 104-5
Vinaigrette:
    lemon Dijon, 165
    lemon parsley, 148

W

Watercress, cream soup, 56-57
Wontons, dumplings, 70-71

Y

Yakitori, 74
Yogurt:
    chicken tikka, 124
    cucumber and mint salad, 174
    mango lassi, 182
    tzatziki, 114-15

Z

Zucchini:
    ratatouille, 160-61
    scallops wrapped in bacon and, 69
    vegetable and chèvre terrine, 76-77